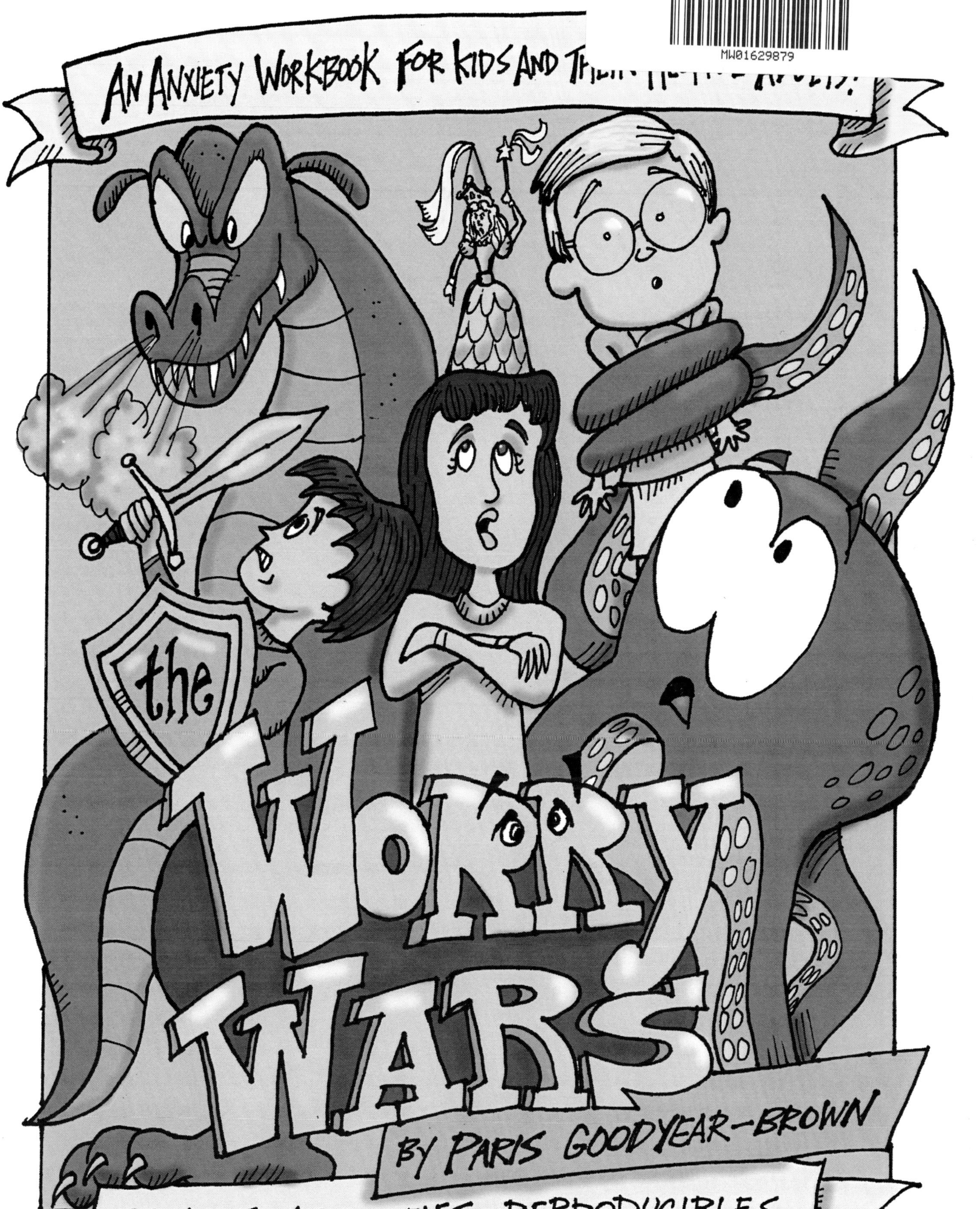
AN ANXIETY WORKBOOK FOR KIDS AND
the
WORRY
WARS
BY PARIS GOODYEAR-BROWN
STORIES • ACTIVITIES • REPRODUCIBLES

DEDICATION

For the one who taught me how to fight my own worry wars.

SPECIAL THANKS

Special thanks to Brian Hull for his amazing illustrations and to my husband for the untold number of hours spent tweaking the layout. Thanks also to my son, Sam, my daughter, Madison, and the cul-de-sac kids who served as my focus group for this project.

The Worry Wars: An Anxiety Workbook for Kids and Their Helpful Adults

ISBN: 978-0-9826606-0-7

Contents

THE BATTLES

The Worry Wars

This versatile workbook offers myriad metaphors, weapons and battle plans for children and their helpful adults to choose from while fighting the Worry Wars. While there is no one cookie-cutter approach that will work for all children in reducing anxiety, a set of best practices exist that inform the interventions suggested in this workbook. This workbook takes children and their helpful adults step by step through the process of bossing back their worries while leaving plenty of room for how this journey might take shape with different kinds of children and different types of anxiety. The phrase "helpful adult" includes counselors, therapists and teachers but is also meant to invite parents to implement these strategies with their children.

The clinical presentation of children with anxiety disorders varies depending on the specific brand of anxiety with which the child struggles. The diagnostic range of worry-related disorders includes post-traumatic stress disorder (PTSD), generalized anxiety disorder (GAD), separation anxiety disorder (SAD, obsessive-compulsive disorder (OCD), specific phobia, selective mutism and more. Children who suffer from any of these diagnoses will find relief from the pages of this book.

Parents may also use this resource with children who don't meet full diagnostic criteria, but just seem to worry a lot. The initial section of the book, The Metaphors, includes several stories that characterize the worry in different ways. In the second section of the book, The Weapons, the therapist and the child together can choose the weapons that will be most meaningful to that child in combatting his worries. The third section of the book, The Battles, presents several fun, child friendly ways to help a child create an exposure hierarchy and record their success as they boss back the worry.

The Metaphors

Anxiety is a symptom that can be very difficult for children to fight on their own. The physiological arousal and the troublesome thoughts that make up an anxiety response can easily overwhelm a child, making him feel out of control. Children can benefit from giving the anxiety a shape, a form. Anxiety with skin on becomes an enemy that can be fought, an irritant that must be silenced, or a creature who can be soothed.

Three separate stories are included, each complete with a child hero with which clients will identify, personifications of the worry, and strategies for regaining control over the worries. In each story, the child hero wins his or her particular worry war. The tale of Daniel the Dragon Slayer depicts the worry as a dragon. This story is the most versatile and can be used in treating any of the anxiety disorders. Polly vs. Princess Perfect is a story geared for high achieving children who struggle with perfectionism, and can also be helpful with obsessive-compulsive behaviors. Oscar vs. Clyde, the Clinging Octopus will appeal to children who struggle with separation anxiety. Read the child whichever story is the best match for his or her developmental age, gender and specific symptomatology. Or read the child all three and talk about the themes across the stories that helped the heros beat back the anxiety.

The Weapons

There are certain steps that all children must take in regaining control of their worries. The first step is to know their enemy. Several activities are included that help a child 1) articulate his unique set of worries, 2) describe how these worries show up in his physical body, and 3) identify his/her anxiety producing thoughts. A variety of practical strategies for fighting the physiological response are offered. Activities aimed at increasing a child's positive coping, decreasing a child's stress response, and containing the worried thoughts are offered.

Once the helpful adult has chosen the initial story and identified a metaphoric enemy, a variety of concrete weapons are offered to fight that enemy. For example, if Daniel the Dragon Slayer has been chosen as the guiding metaphoric story, the the sword, the shield and/or the fire extinguisher can be used as the weapons with which the child will fight his worries. Each template can be personalized with a child's own cognitive restructuring statements, boss back talk and/or coping strategies. The finished products can be cut out, decorated and taken home as tangible reminders of the strategies that children can use in their battles. Full sized reproducibles of the story's heros and nemeses are included. These can be photocopied, made into puppets and used in role plays to practice the strategies needed to boss back the worries.

The graphic of the bulging bicep followed by the words "Getting Stronger" signals experiential activities that will help the child develop his own worry workout. Relaxation skills, coping thoughts and positive self-talk must all be practiced for the child to get strong enough to successfully complete the battles described in the third section of this workbook.

The Battles

Once a child has chosen a metaphor to characterize the anxiety and developed the necessary weapons to fight it, all that is left are the series of battles that will lead the child to victory. The evidence base for the treatment of anxiety disorders suggests that gradual exposure to the anxiety provoking stimuli is necessary for significant change to occur. Exposures can be titrated carefully through the creation of an exposure hierarchy. Several tools are offered in the third section of this book that help to structure both the design and the completion of such hierarchies in ways that will appeal to children.

Included in this section are tools for monitoring the child's subjective units of distress (SUD) prior to and following an exposure to the anxiety. As the child becomes aware of how bad he feels just prior to completing an exposure and soon after the exposure is completed, he can gain powerful knowledge about how anxiety works and how to push ahead even when he feels his worst.

Children who struggle with anxiety often have a hard time seeing their progress. They need parents, teachers and counselors to function as cheerleaders and coaches for them. The tools in this section offer ways of mapping a child's progress in their fight to take back ground that has been dominated by worry. Some children may respond best to the staircase or the ladder template. Each exposure is written on a step or rung and rewards are given each time a new level is achieved. Some children may choose to copy the full page version of the dragon, Princess Perfect or the octopus and then manipulate these symbols. Other children will want to create their own characters to symbolize their worries. They may want to rip off pieces of their chosen icons each time they successfully complete an exposure. They may choose to use the paper bricks to cover up their symbol, brick by brick, as they complete each exposure. The most important part is that they see their own progress.

The Battle Plans

1. Choose the story that fits most closely with the kind of anxiety with which the child in your care struggles.

2. Choose the templates that match the story. Use these to record worried talk and to generate, record and practice boss back statements. Help the child become proficient at using the other weapons in section 2, including implementing positive coping strategies, relaxation exercises and thought stopping techniques.

3. Use the pyramid to create a set of exposures. Start with an exposure that will be easy for the child to complete. Then move up the hierarchy, helping the child acquire mastery at each level.

4. Choose a template to record the child's successes and give rewards for each success.

5. Celebrate the child's victory with a graduation celebration.

THE METAPHORS

DANIEL
the
DRAGON
SLAYER

Daniel was not always a Dragon Slayer. He started out as a regular kid. He went to school all week, played soccer on Saturdays, and built amazing creatures in his spare time.

He got mad at his sister, sad when it rained and was sometimes scared of the dark. But he was a pretty happy kid.

Then one day he was playing in the living room while his mom listened to the news. He half-listened to a report about a museum opening, another about an earthquake in Asia, and a third about the local hockey team's big win over the weekend.

That night Daniel's mom tucked him in as usual and gave him a kiss. It seemed like a normal night. The only difference was, a dragon egg had appeared under Daniel's bed.

Daniel the Dragon Slayer

As he lay in his bed, he began to think about the earthquake he had heard about on the news. He wondered if an earthquake could happen in his town. He wondered if his house was made to stand up under that kind of shaking.

As he turned these thoughts over in his mind, the egg began to crack. He decided that if an earthquake happened while he was sleeping, he'd be safest if he had pillows all around him, so he spent some time arranging things just so.

Daniel the Dragon Slayer

Once the pillows were piled into a fort, Daniel felt better and was able to go to sleep.

The cracks in the egg got bigger.

In the morning, Daniel woke up feeling good. He got ready for school and walked down to the bus stop. As he waited for the bus, he thought again about the earthquake. If there was an earthquake and the road cracked, the bus could fall in. Maybe walking to school would be safer.

Finally he decided not to get on the bus. He started walking to school, and he felt better.

In his backpack, the baby dragon quietly pushed his way out of the egg.

Daniel the Dragon Slayer

Over the next couple of weeks, Daniel spent more and more time worrying about earthquakes and doing little things that made him feel better. The dragon, unnoticed at first, seemed to grow with each thing that Daniel did.

The dragon began to talk to Daniel directly. He would say things like "What if the roof fell down on top of you?" So, Daniel put on a helmet. He felt better.

The dragon got bigger.

Daniel the Dragon Slayer

But when he went to school, his friends called him "Helmet Head." Then he worried about being called names. The dragon got bigger. The dragon said, "What if your friends don't like you anymore?" So Daniel pretended to be sick and stayed home from school.

It was then that the dragon breathed his first fiery breath.

Daniel the Dragon Slayer

Daniel decided that he was in trouble. He realized that when he listened to the dragon, the dragon got bigger. When he did things to drown out the dragon's voice, he felt better ... but only for a minute. Listening to the dragon's worried talk fed the dragon. The more attention he paid to the worries, the larger the dragon got.

Daniel decided he must cut off the dragon's food supply. As scary as it felt, *he had to stop doing the things the dragon told him to do*. From now on, Daniel would take the bus to school, even though it made him feel sick. He would not wear the helmet even though he felt safer with it on. He would not be the dragon's slave anymore.

Daniel the Dragon Slayer

He began to listen to what the dragon said in a new way and planned some things he would say to boss back the dragon. He spent some time fashioning a sword and a shield.

The next time the dragon said, "What if an earthquake happens here?" Daniel raised his shield, brandished his sword and yelled back, "Earthquakes don't happen around here!"

Daniel the Dragon Slayer

The first time Daniel talked back to the dragon, the dragon was shocked into silence. Then the dragon got louder and his breath got hotter. Daniel knew that this meant war. Daniel knew the dragon wanted him to back down, but he was sick and tired of worrying. He raced down the hall and pulled the fire extinguisher from the wall, the dragon fast on his heels. Daniel whipped around, shouting,

"You are a liar and I don't have to listen to you!
LEAVE ME ALONE!"

Daniel the Dragon Slayer

This blast of truth—well, the truth and some white, foamy stuff—quenched the dragon's fiery breath once and for all. As the dragon skulked away, Daniel knew he had won the war.

Daniel went back to playing soccer on Saturdays and building swamp creatures in front of the TV. But he always kept his weapons nearby ...

Daniel the Dragon Slayer

... so that if the dragon ever tried to return, he would be ready.

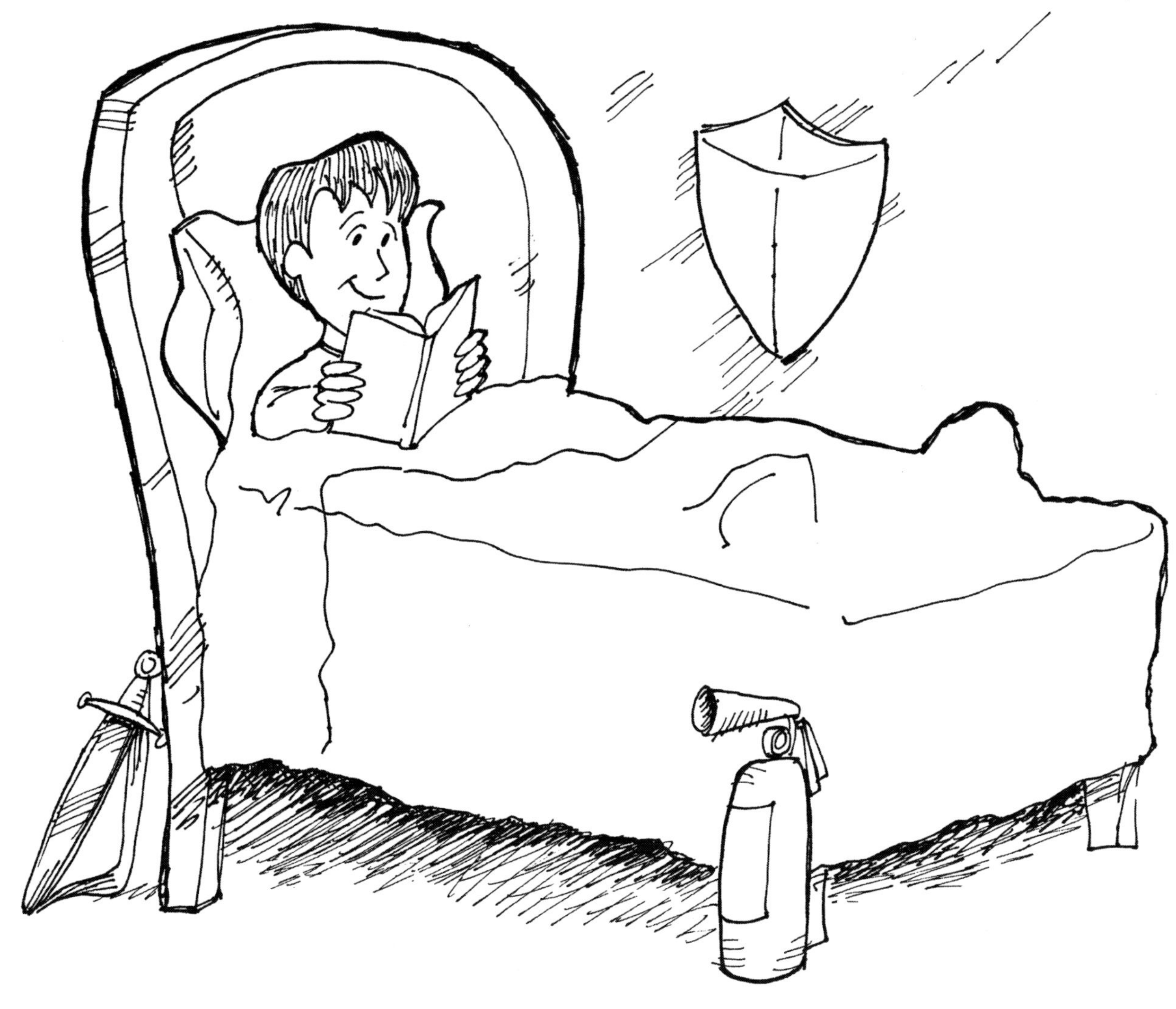

POLLY
VERSUS
Princess
Perfect

Polly was good at lots of things. She could hit the high notes when she sang, play the piano like a pro, and draw a star without picking up her marker. She made her bed without being reminded. She was the girl that all the other girls followed in ballet class. She scored so often on the soccer field that her coach kept her in most of the game.

In her class, kids came to her for help with their math. People complimented Polly on her hair, on her voice, on her artwork. When people said nice things to her, she smiled and said thank you.

She never let on that there was a driving force behind all that goodness.

She never talked about the little voice that came from the general direction of her shoulder, the voice that was getting louder every day and making her more and more unhappy.

Polly Versus Princess Perfect

Polly had always liked getting dressed for school. She took pride in her appearance and had fun picking out what to wear. But lately, every time she wore her favorite tights, the ones with rows and rows of purple and red hearts, she could never get the rows straight enough.

She started getting up early because she needed extra time to make the hearts line up just so. Just when she thought the tights were perfectly arranged, the voice would say, "They're not right yet! They're not perfect!" Polly looked all around but saw no one. So she sighed and started over again on her tights.

A couple of weeks later, Polly decided that she wanted to wear braids to school. As she stood in the mirror admiring her braids, a voice said, "They don't look as good as the ones in the magazine!"

Polly whirled around, sure that the voice had come from behind her. Again, she saw nothing ... but gritting her teeth, she pulled out her braids and started over.

She started getting in trouble with her mom because she wasn't ready to go when it was time to get in the car. There were many unpleasant mornings.

Polly knew she was overreacting, but she didn't know how to stop.

Polly Versus Princess Perfect

Then one day, the same kind of thing happened at school.
The class was making paper hearts to decorate the bulletin
board. She drew a heart and instantly the voice said, "It's
not perfect yet! You can do better than that!" She crumpled
up the paper and drew another heart.

Her classmate leaned over and said, "Cool heart!" Even as
Polly smiled back, the voice said, "What does he know?"
She held back frustrated tears as she ripped up page after
page of hearts. Her teacher, Mrs. Smith,
came over and said, "I think your heart
is lovely!" The voice said,
"She's just saying
that to be nice."

Polly felt like a prisoner. But she wasn't sure how to get free. She decide that the first step was to get a glimpse of her captor. So she waited for an opportunity to catch the owner of that voice. That night, as she was sitting on her bed painting her toenails, the voice returned. She had just finished painting her pinky toe when the voice said, "You missed a spot!"

Polly sneaked a sideways glance at the mirror and, making a quick grab, plucked the little creature off her shoulder.

She stared in suprise at
the beautiful young
lady. "You're a
princess!" Polly
said in suprise.

"That's right.
Princess Perfect at
your service."

"Why are you
bothering me?"
Polly asked.

"Well, if you're
going to do something, you may as well do it right!"

"I'm exhausted trying to do things perfectly. Please leave
me alone."

"I most certainly will not! Look how much better your nails
are now that I helped you!"

"Helped me?! Helped me?! Because of you I never feel like
what I do is good enough. I want you out of here! Go find
another shoulder to sit on."

Polly Versus Princess Perfect

"I think you'll find it harder than you think to get rid of me," Princess Perfect said while smiling sweetly.

That night, Polly waited until her tiny hitchhiker was snoring, plucked the wand out of her hand and hid it in her dresser. She thought the Princess would be powerless without her wand but while her voice was smaller, she was still bossing Polly around.

She knew that the things the Princess was saying were lies, so Polly made a list of things she could say to boss back the Princess.

Polly Versus Princess Perfect

All day Polly practiced these statements over and over again and waited for the Princess to appear. Sure enough, she showed up while Polly was practicing piano. Princess Perfect piped up with, "You missed a note!"

Polly ran to her sister's room and got the weapon she needed.

When Princess Perfect opened her mouth to speak again, Polly yelled through the megaphone ...

Polly Versus Princess Perfect

"IT'S OKAY TO MAKE MISTAKES!"

The reverberations from Polly's amplified voice sent the princess sailing through the picture window. Polly shut the window and locked it.

Polly slept soundly that night for the first time in weeks. In the days to come, Polly would often pause in the middle of a task and listen, but all she could hear ...

... were the blessed sounds of silence.

Oscar and Clyde, the Clinging Octopus

Oscar's parents stood outside the nursery window, oohing and aahing over their newborn baby. He had ten chubby fingers and ten chubby toes. His companion, Clyde, had no fingers and no toes, but had instead eight not-so-chubby tentacles and was very cute in his own right.

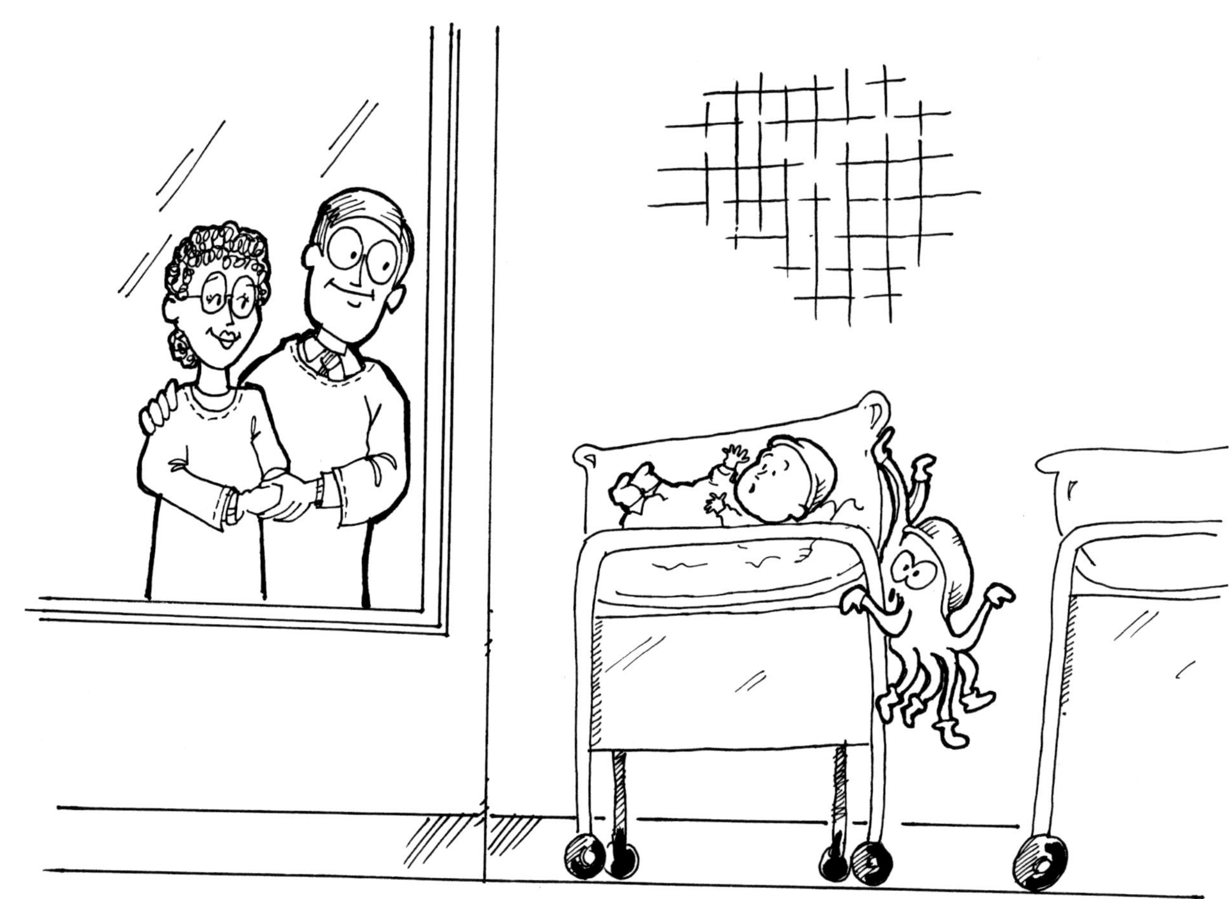

No one oohed and aahed over Clyde though, mainly because, for whatever reason, they could not see him.

Oscar And Clyde, The Clinging Octopus

When it was time to take Oscar home from the hospital, Clyde tagged along for the ride.

His parents fussed over Oscar's seat belt, and Clyde held on tight.

When they arrived at the house, Oscar was ushered into his new room, complete with a super-duper rocking chair and a sparkling new crib.

Clyde, unnoticed, found his own place to sleep.

As Oscar grew, so did Clyde.

Oscar liked to play hide-and-seek, but Clyde didn't like being too far away from mommy.

So he persuaded Oscar to hide in places that were pretty easy to find.

Oscar And Clyde, The Clinging Octopus

Oscar liked to ride his tricycle, but Clyde didn't like being too far from the house, so he made sure that Oscar stuck pretty close, even though it left Oscar a little dizzy.

Clyde was happiest when he and Oscar were playing near mommy. When Oscar couldn't see mom, Clyde helped him make up excuses to check on mom a lot ...

Oscar was getting sick of Clyde's clinginess, but wasn't sure what to do about it.

Oscar And Clyde, The Clinging Octopus

When the day finally came for Oscar to start preschool, Clyde was not ready. All the way to school, Clyde clung to the roof of the car and went over all the reasons why Oscar should stay home with mommy.

Oscar And Clyde, The Clinging Octopus

Oscar tried not to listen, but Clyde was hard to ignore and by the time they got to school, Oscar was feeling sick.

At school, Oscar's mom walked him to the door of his classroom. She squatted down and gave him a big hug, but when she tried to stand back up, she found that she was squeezed tight. She was suprised at the strength of his hold and the number of tears.

Mom gave up and took him home, saying, "We'll try again tomorrow."

Back at the house, Clyde fell asleep and Oscar finally got some peace. Oscar wondered what he was missing at preschool. The sand and water table had looked pretty fun, and he had seen a twisty slide out on the playground.

That night, as Oscar snuggled with mom to read a book, he remembered the whole shelf of books he had seen in the preschool room. He decided that he would definitely stay at preschool tomorrow.

Oscar And Clyde, The Clinging Octopus

In the morning, Clyde started in with his worried talk. Oscar rolled up the windows to shut out Clyde's voice. Clyde got so upset he inked himself, and the What Ifs dripped down the car window.

Oscar And Clyde, The Clinging Octopus

This time Clyde got so scared while Oscar and his mom were saying goodbye that one of his tentacles squeezed convulsively around Oscar's neck.

Oscar started gasping for air and mom, seeing his troubled breathing, sighed, patted him on the back and took him home again.

As Clyde calmed down, he loosened his grip. As Oscar got his breath back, he realized that every time he listened to Clyde, he allowed Clyde to be large and in charge. He had let Clyde be the boss for years. It had just seemed easier than fighting. He would have to work hard to change things, but now he had a good reason.

Oscar had seen the paintings made by the other kids at preschool. He loved painting. He had also seen the big jar of Goldfish. He loved Goldfish. He asked mom for Goldfish when they got home, but she didn't have any. Oscar decided that he was definitely going to preschool tomorrow.

Oscar And Clyde, The Clinging Octopus

But what to do about Clyde? Clyde wasn't trying to ruin his life, but he was ruining it just the same. Oscar knew he needed ammunition to fight Clyde's worry talk, so he practiced some things he could say to show Clyde who was the boss.

When Clyde said, "What if something happens to her?" Oscar would say, "She'll be fine!"

When Clyde said, "What if you don't like it?" Oscar would say, "I'll have fun!"

When Clyde said, "What if she never comes back?" Oscar would say, "She will come back!"

Oscar chiseled these boss back words onto bricks and stacked them up in the car.

Oscar And Clyde, The Clinging Octopus

On the way to school the next morning, whenever Clyde threw out a What If, Oscar talked back to him while pinning down a tentacle with one of his bricks. When they got to school, Oscar got out of the car footloose and fancy free, while Clyde remained pinned to the top of the car.

Oscar And Clyde, The Clinging Octopus

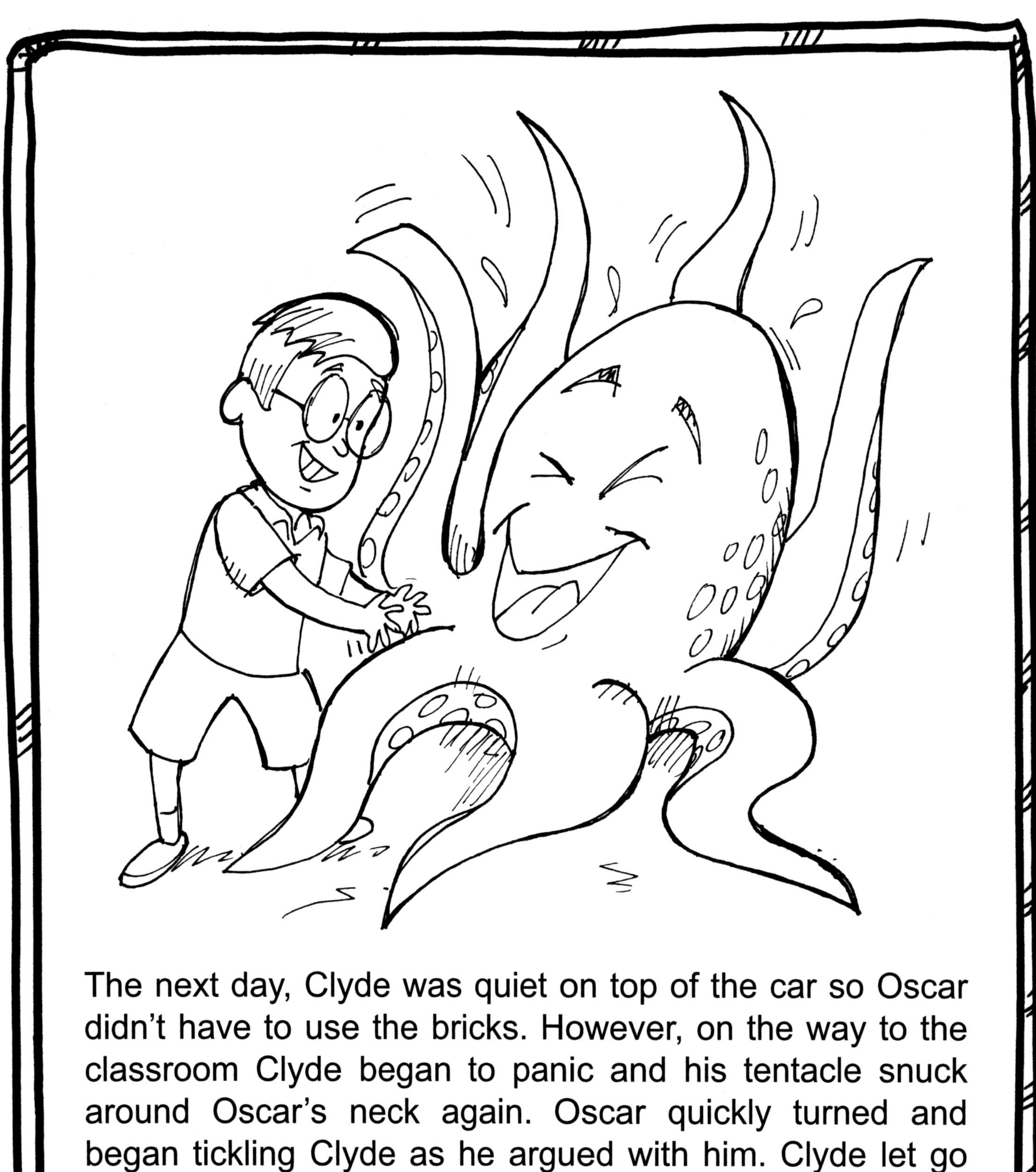

The next day, Clyde was quiet on top of the car so Oscar didn't have to use the bricks. However, on the way to the classroom Clyde began to panic and his tentacle snuck around Oscar's neck again. Oscar quickly turned and began tickling Clyde as he argued with him. Clyde let go and collapsed in a giggling heap.

Oscar And Clyde, The Clinging Octopus

The next day Clyde was quiet on the way to school and kept his tentacles to himself in the hallway. However, when Oscar's mom went to give him a hug, Clyde's tentacles began to reach out, but Oscar was ready. He tied two tentacles together while he used his boss back words. Then he tied another two together. In the end, Clyde looked like a pretzel. In a final effort to show Clyde who was really boss, Oscar whipped out the duck tape and put a piece firmly over his mouth.

Clyde watched quietly all day as Oscar ate his Goldfish, read his books and played on the twisty slide outside with new friends. At the end of the day Oscar scooped Clyde up and took him home.

Oscar And Clyde, The Clinging Octopus

Clyde had seen that preschool wasn't so bad and agreed to behave himself from that day forward. After that, Clyde and Oscar got along beautifully.

Oscar even let Clyde sit next to him in the car
on the way to school.

Oscar And Clyde, The Clinging Octopus

THE WEAPONS

What is worry?

One valuable weapon in any war is understanding how your enemy works. In this war, your enemy is too much worry.

Worry is a bad, upset feeling that you have on the inside. Some people call this feeling "stress", "anxiety", "fear" or describe it as "feeling nervous", but to make things simple we're going to use the word worry.

Everybody worries. Worry works like an alarm that goes off in your brain, an early warning system to signal you that danger is nearby. This works great when there really is danger nearby.

Imagine that you are getting ready to cross the street. Just as you put your foot down, you hear a big truck coming towards you fast! Your brain trips your alarm, which tells your body to jump back from the road ... and you escape unharmed. Your alarm keeps you safe. Once you're safe, the alarm turns off, your heart rate slows down and you feel calm again.

Learning to hit the snooze!

Sometimes, though, the alarm gets stuck! It may go off even when there is no real danger. You start worrying about things that "might be" when there is no real threat.

Worry can make you feel sick inside, and it can take up so much of your time that you don't get to enjoy being a kid! The good news is that you can learn how to turn off the alarm. The weapons in this section help you learn and practice hitting the snooze button. As you get stronger and learn to fight the Worry Wars, you will retrain your alarm.

The Worry Worms

The first step to being able to fight your worries is to identify them and talk about them with a helpful adult. Worries are like worms, they can be wriggly and hard to pin down. Use the worms on the opposite page to write down your worries.

Getting *Stronger*

Adult hides rubber worms all around the room and plays a game of "hot and cold" with the child to help him find the worms. Each time he finds a worm, he talks about another one of his worries. Each worry is written on a worm on the opposite page.

The Worry Worms

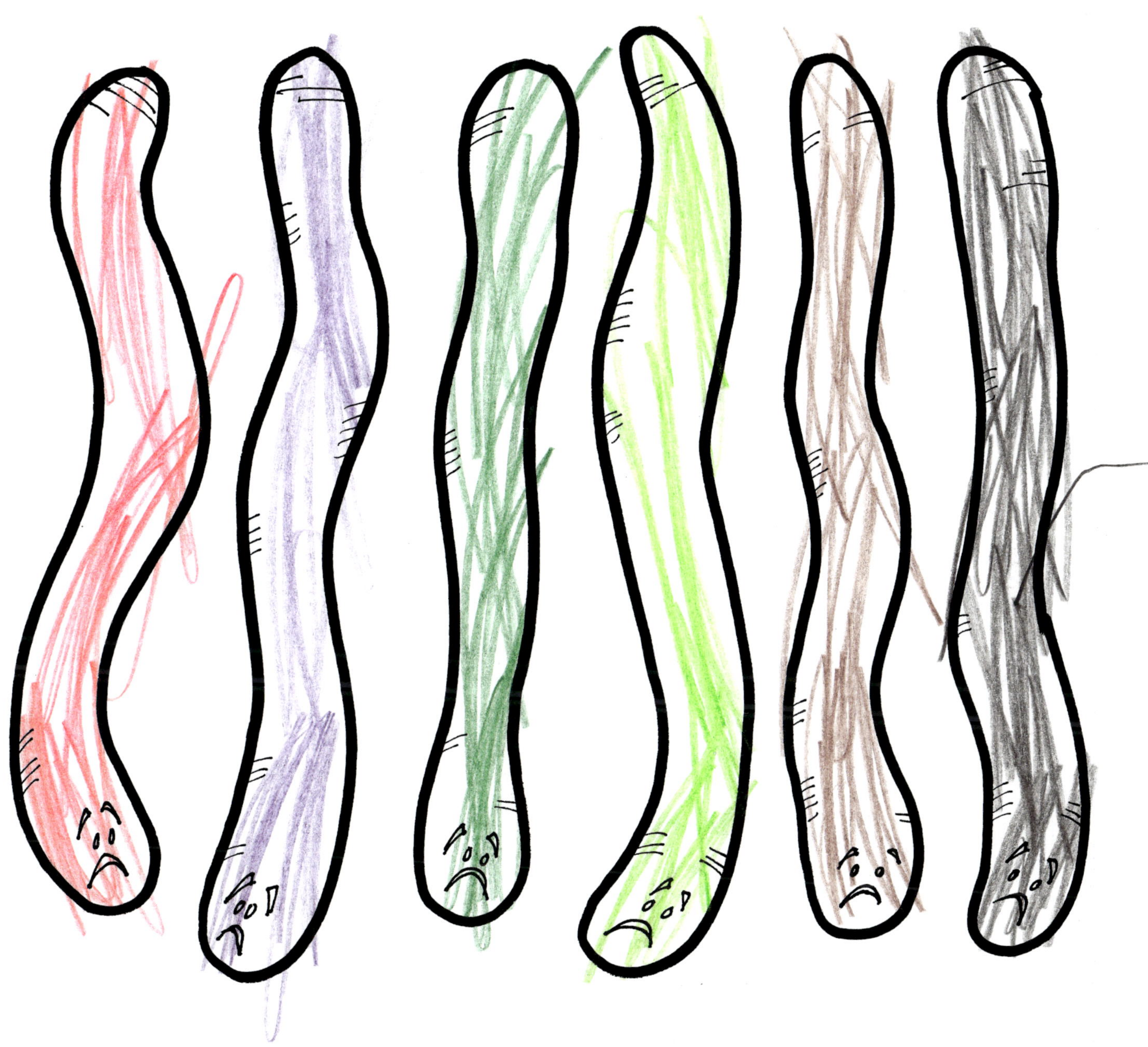

Can of Worms

Great job pinpointing your worries! Worries, like worms, will try to wriggle into every part of your life. They can wriggle out and take over even when you're trying to have fun or do your homework. Let's create a special container for storing your worry worms. Once you put the worries in there, they will stay put until you decide you are ready to deal with them. As you learn how to fight the worries, you can take them out one at a time and get rid of them.

Getting *Stronger*

Find an empty Pringles can (be sure to keep the plastic lid. Cover the can with construction paper and write messages on it, such as "Stay put!" or "Must have permission to open", or draw pictures. Put the completed worry worms from the previous page into the container. Take eah worm out one at a time when you are ready to deal with them.

Can of Worms

Physical Cues

How does your body tell you it's worried?

Your body gives you signals when you are starting to worry. If you can learn to notice those signals, you can begin fighting the worry right away!

Physical Cues

Our bodies sound the alarm when we begin to feel anxious. Cut out all the cues that your body gives you and glue them on the boy's body.

Physical Cues

How does your body tell you it's worried?

Your body gives you signals when you are starting to worry. If you can learn to notice those signals, you can begin fighting the worry right away!

Physical Cues

Our bodies sound the alarm when we begin to feel anxious. Cut out all the cues that your body gives you and glue them on the girl's body.

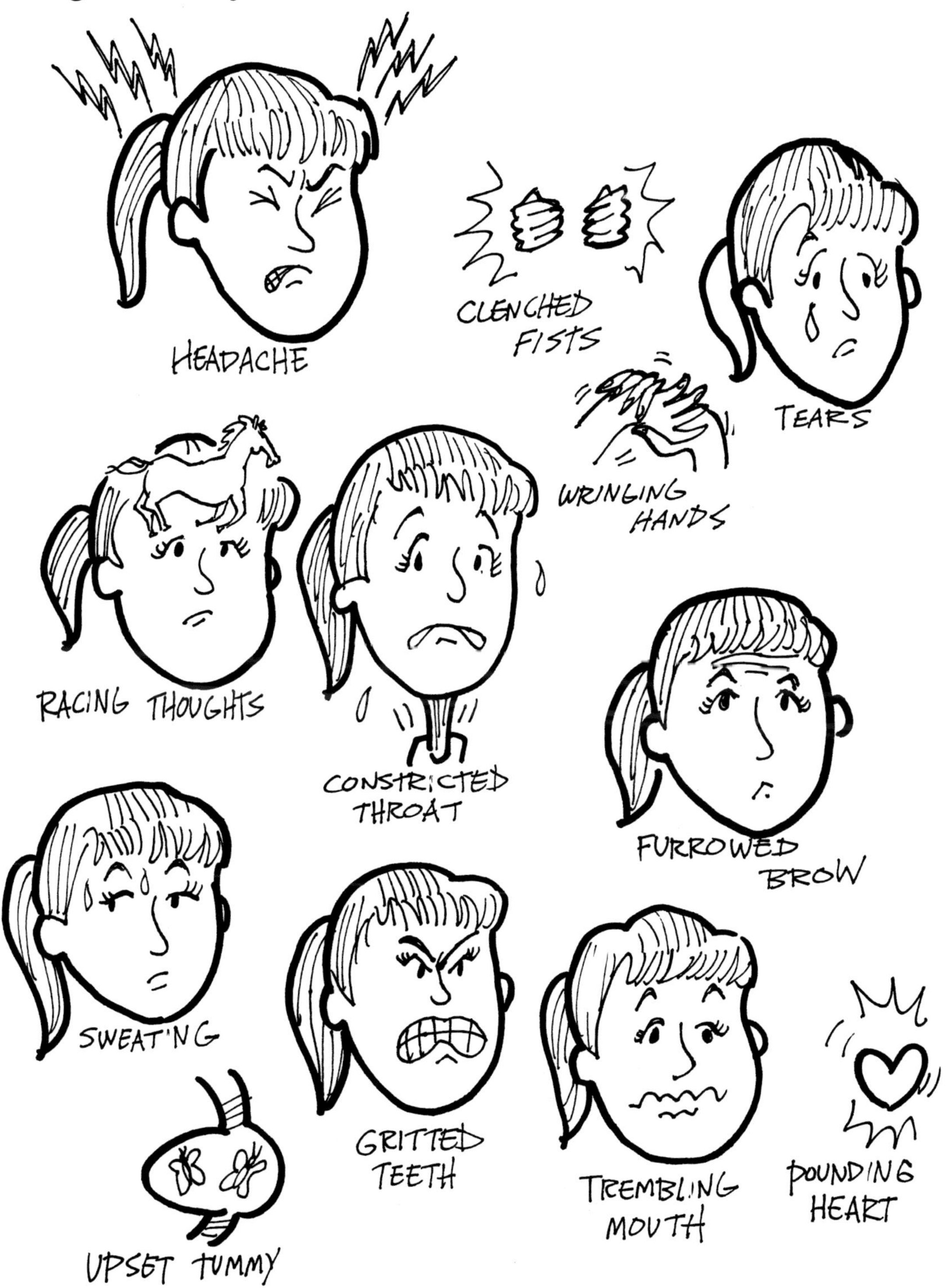

Creating Copecakes

You have lots of choices about what to do when your worries start to bother you. Some kids go into their rooms, shut their doors, sit on their beds and worry alone. Other kids repeat their worries over and over again to a helpful adult, but the telling doesn't actually make them feel better. Some kids sing along with the radio or go play soccer or pick a fight.

How you cope with your worries can make them feel bigger or smaller. The good news is that there are certain ingredients that go into a good coping strategy. For example, a coping strategy that brings you closer to people usually helps more than one that pulls you away from people. Helpful coping strategies should:

1. Be good for you.
2. Be good for others.
3. Be easy to do.
4. Make you feel better.

When you are worried, you may yell at your parents. Yelling is not good for others, so this coping choice needs to be replaced. Eating too much candy is another way to cope, but is not good for your body. Going on a trip to Disneyworld might make you feel better, but it's not easy to do. Playing a board game or riding your bike has all the right ingredients. The mixer on the opposite page has four prongs. Write in the four ingredients that make for helpful coping strategies.

Copecakes Mixer

Cooking Copecakes

Once you have decided on the best ingredients for your coping choices, you can experiment with lots of different ideas and see what helps the most.

Use the baking tin on the opposite page to write down healthy choices you can make to cope while you're learning to talk back to your worried thoughts. Let them cook for awhile and see which ones you like the best. Try to use each coping strategy at least three times. Then you and your helpful adult can talk about which ones helped the most.

Copecake Baking Tin

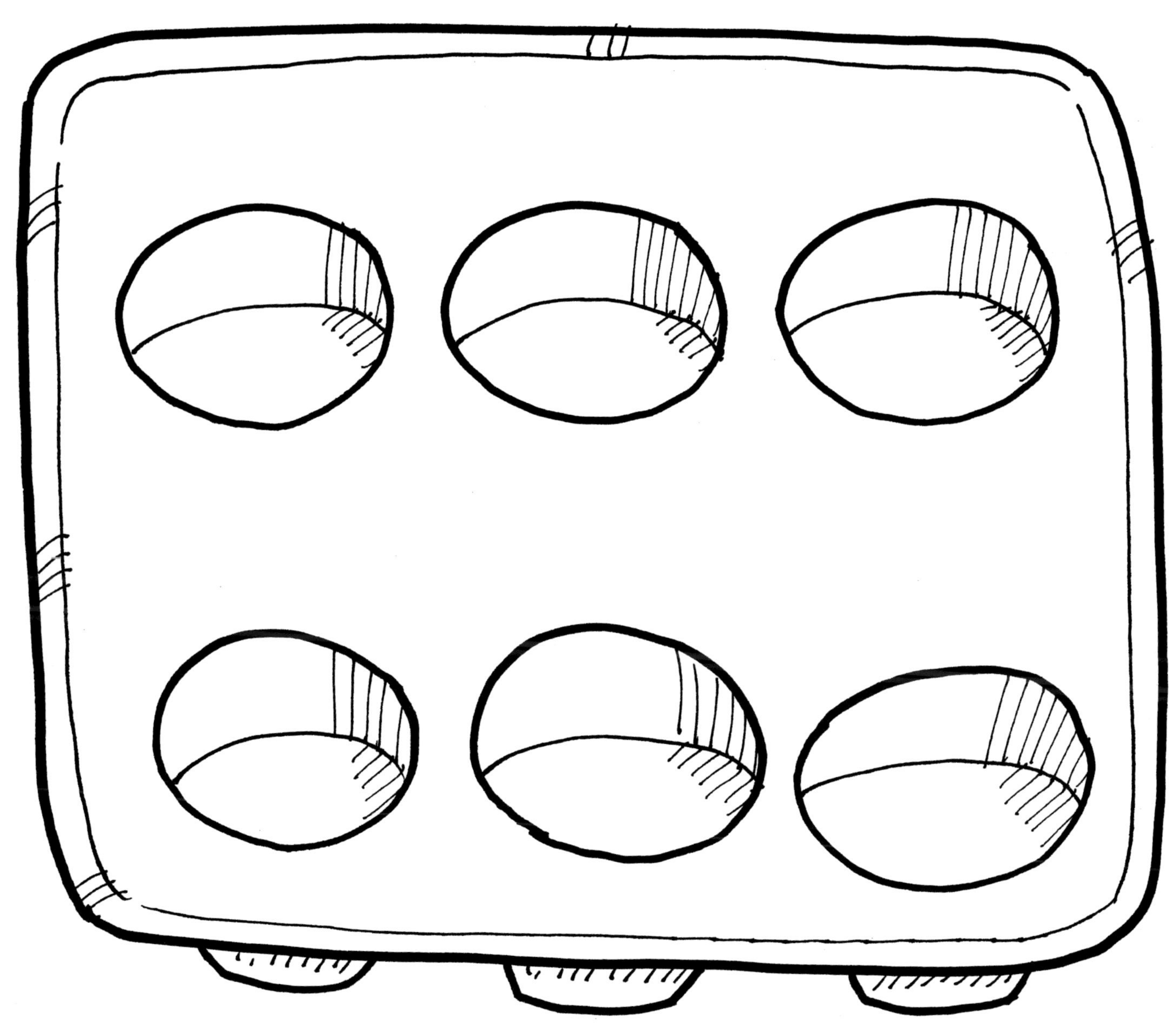

Cool Copecakes

You've spent some time trying out different things you can do to cope. You've probably found that some of them work well and others don't make much of a difference.

Write down the coping behaviors that make you feel the best on the opposite page. Cut them out and decorate them. Then take them home and put them in a place where you can see them and be reminded of ways to help yourself feel better when your worries trip your alarm.

Copecakes

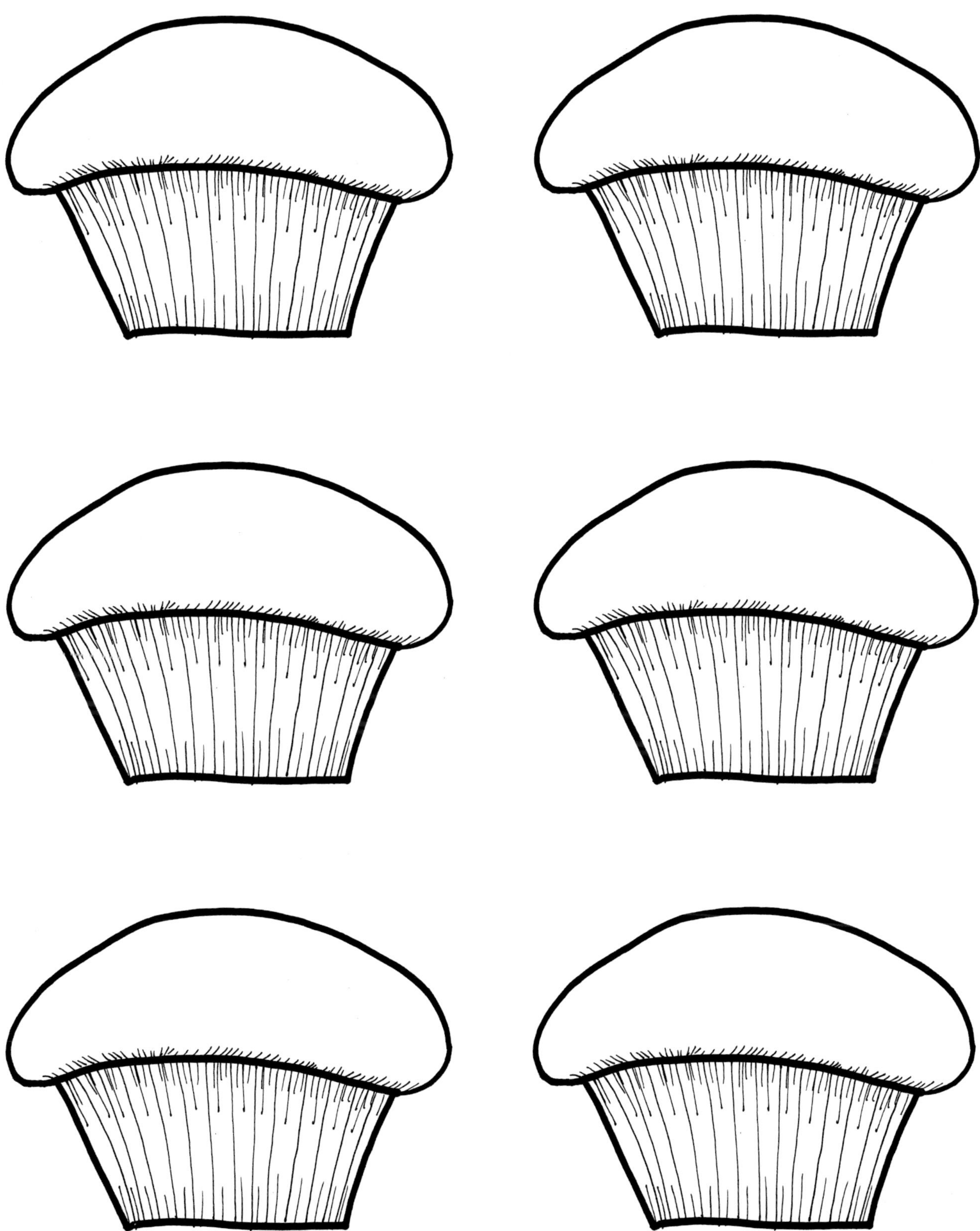

Gathering a Team

One powerful weapon that can help you to fight the worry is the people around you. Different people do different kinds of things that make you feel good. Using the list on the next page, color in the paper dolls to look like different people. Write their names on the sashes that cross their bodies.

Gathering a Team

Name one person (or more) who ...
- gives you food, clothing and shelter
- encourages you
- teaches you new things
- gives you a hug/kiss/handshake/pat on the back
- protects you
- makes you feel safe and relaxed
- is fun to play with
- gives you compliments

Team Member Bookmark

When you are battling your worries, it helps to be reminded of the special people on your team. On the opposite page is a blank bookmark. Copy it as many times as you like, cut out the bookmarks and make one for each of the special people on your team.

Color in the body and write the name in the space provided. In the bottom of the bookmark, write in one nice thing that your special person says or does that helps you fight your worries.

Team Member Bookmark

Bubble Breathing

Bubbles can be a great way to help you practice your breathing. Make sure you have plenty of bubbles and try the three exercises below.

Hold a full bubble wand in front of your mouth.

Exercise One

Take a shallow breath in and release it quickly.
You probably only get a few bubbles.

Exercise Two

Take a deep breath in and blow out hard and fast.
You may make lots of little bubbles.

Exercise Three

Now, take a deep breath in and let it out slowly, so slowly that you almost can't hear your own breath being released. What happened? Did you make a big bubble?

With practice, you can use the third method to make *gigantic* bubbles. Taking deep, controlled breaths is one way to tell your body to calm down. Blowing huge bubbles helps.

Bubble Breathing

Practice making three gigantic bubbles at least once each day.

Pinwheels

Pinwheels don't seem very scary, but they can become another powerful weapon when used to train your body to calm down by taking deep belly breaths. Pinwheels come in all shapes and sizes. Choose one that you like and then try the following exercise.

Hold the pinwheel close to your lips and make it spin. That wasn't very hard, was it?

Now hold the pinwheel as far out in front of you as your arm will reach and make the pinwheel spin. That was a lot harder, wasn't it? It takes a much deeper breath the second time.

Pinwheels

Make your own pinwheel by copying this pinwheel onto thick paper and folding over the edges. On each blade, you can draw pictures or add words that help you feel calm and content.

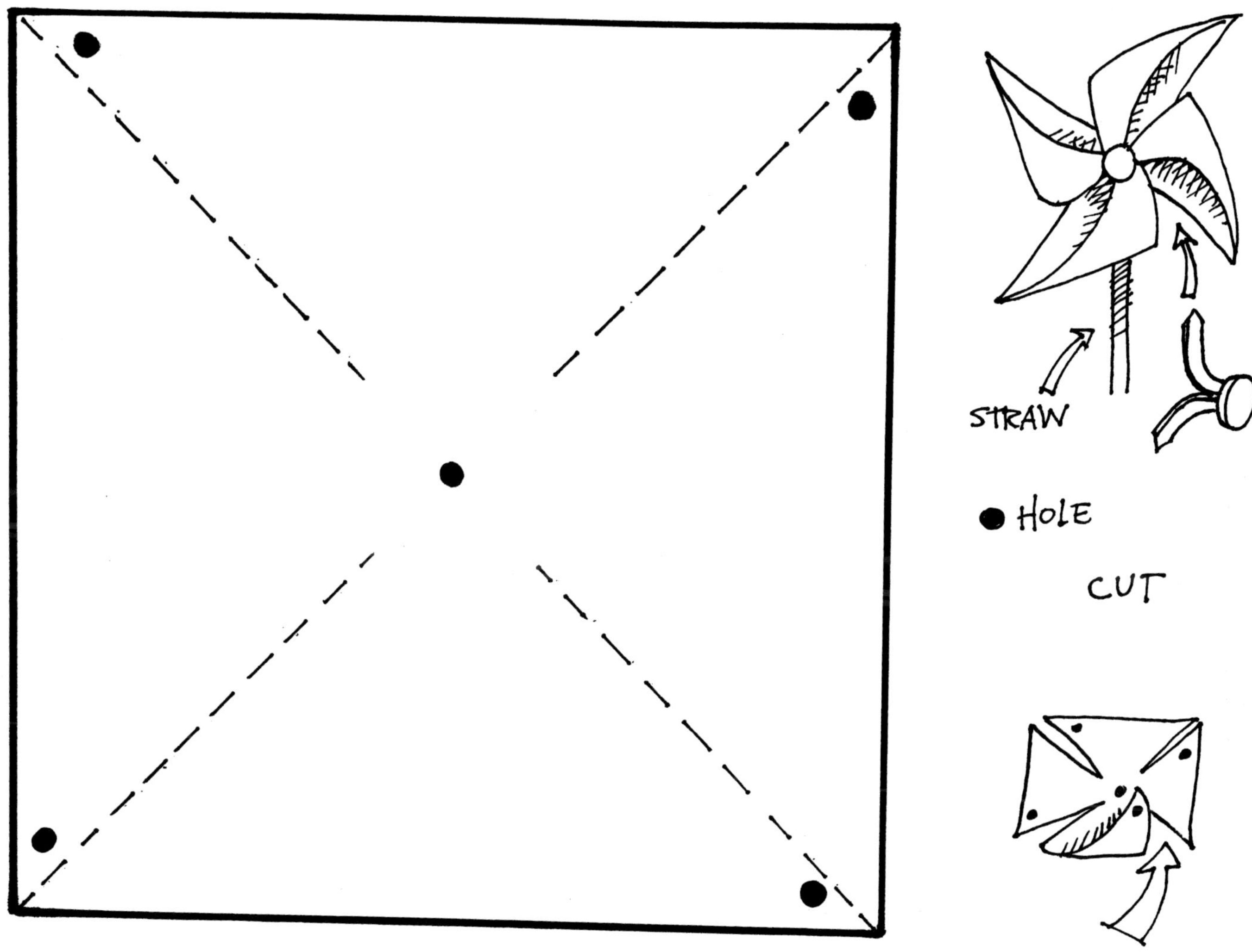

Star Breathing

Ever draw a star before? It's not hard when you've got a guide. It's also handy since the time it takes to get to each of the five points on your star allows your body time to take a long slow breath in. As your pencil moves from point to point, it's liking ticking off seconds on a clock.

Trace each of the three stars below. You'll draw a deep breath in as you draw the first star, hold your breath as you draw the second star, and gently, slowly let your breath out as you trace the third star.

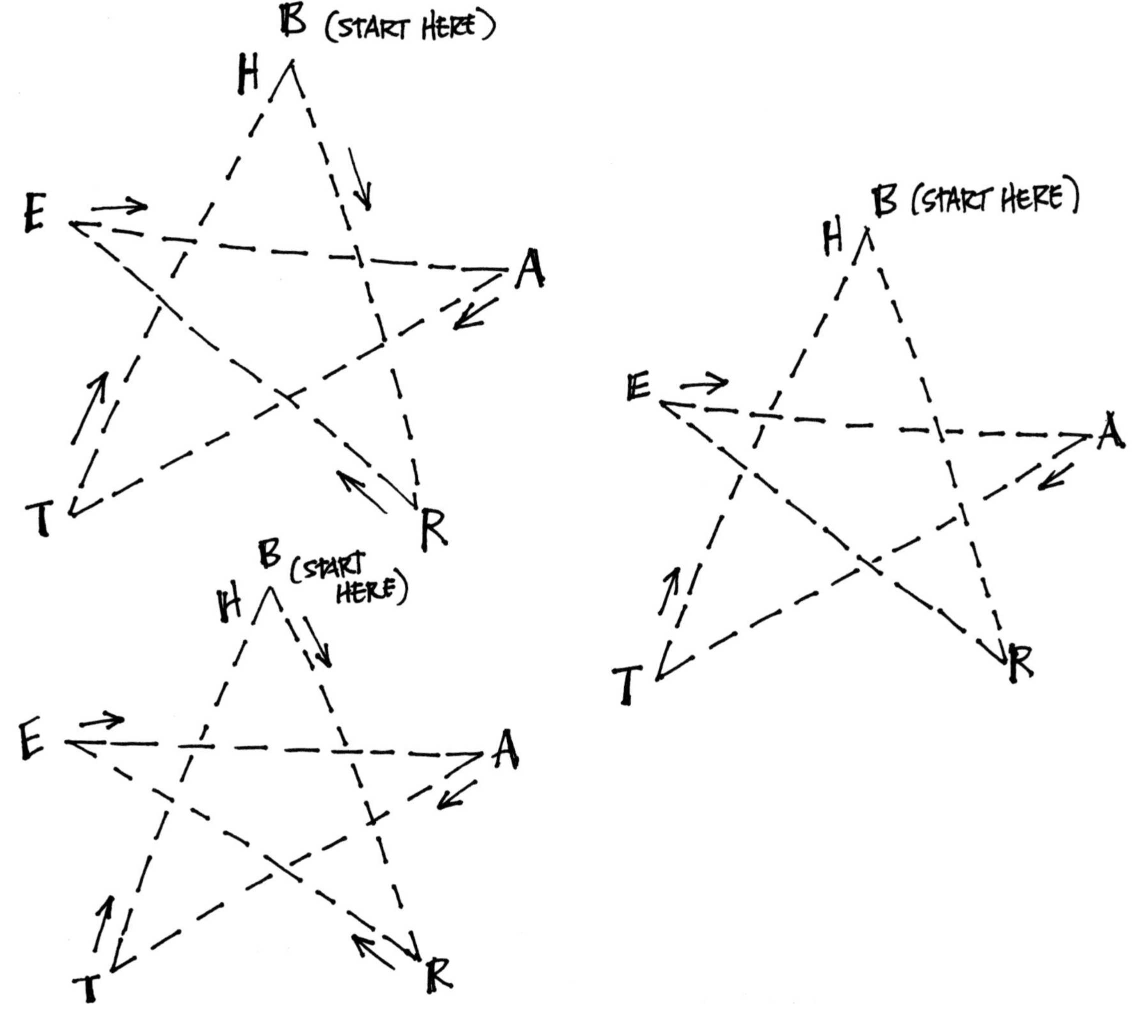

Star Breathing

Here's another way to use the star to practice your breathing. Put your pencil on point A. Breathe in as you draw the line, hold your breath briefly as you make the point, and exhale as you draw the next line. Then start all over again.

You can cut out these stars, decorate them and put them in your room to help guide your breathing as you're falling asleep.

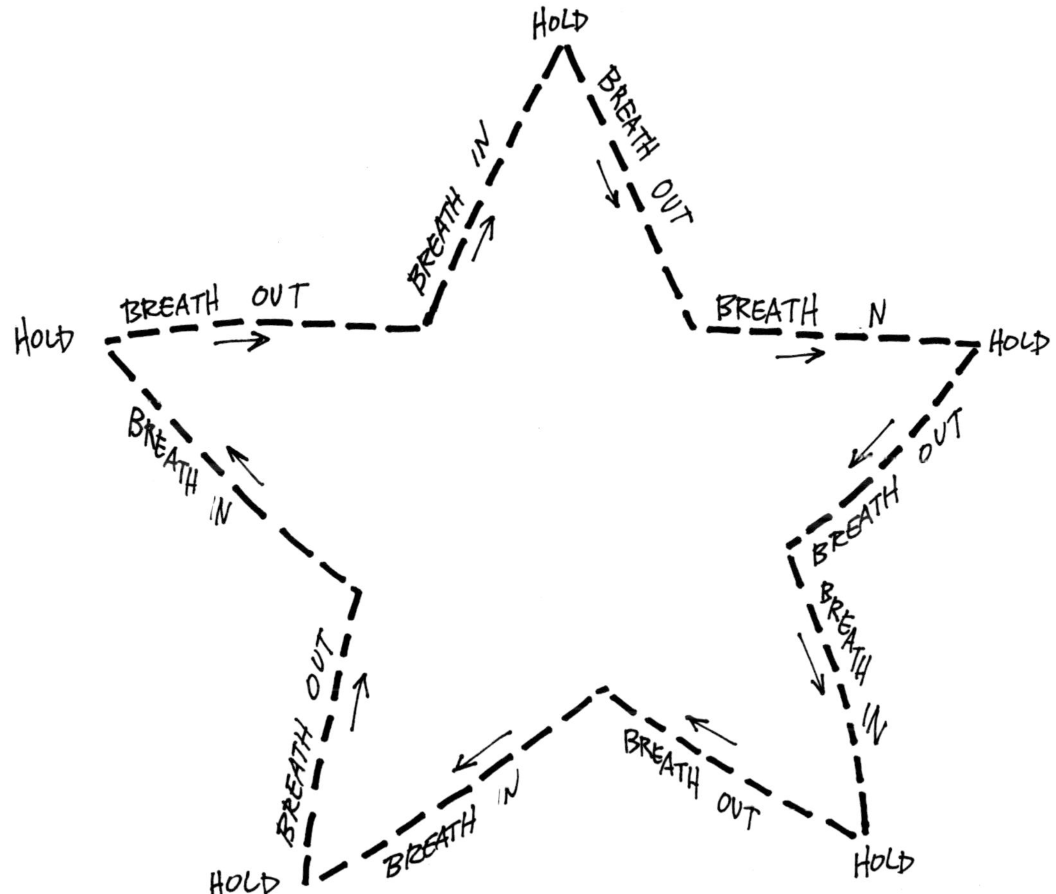

Just an idea ...

Purchase glow in the dark stars and put them above the child's bed. Parents can snuggle with the child at bedtime and practice the star breathing together.

My Chillin' Place

Draw a picture of a place where you could feel safe and happy, a place where you can just chill out. It might be a place you have visited, or it might be a made-up place. When you start to feel worried, imagine that you are there.

Picture Perfect Postcard

Thinking about fun things that could happen in the future can help you fight your worries. Choose a fun or beautiful place that you would like to visit. Then imagine that you are already there.

Write a postcard to a friend or family member from your special place. On the front you can write the address and a few words telling what it's like in the neat place you are visiting. On the back, draw a picture.

I chill with my iPod

Music can be a powerful weapon. When we listen to music, we usually have a feeling reaction. Some songs make us feel better and others can make us feel worse. Have you ever listened to a song that made you feel sad? How about scared? Happy? Calm?

You can choose certain music to listen to while you are getting strong enough to fight your worries. On the page opposite, write the names of three songs that make you feel happy and three songs that help you feel calm.

Getting *Stronger*

Worries can bother you the most during down times like when you're riding in the car or laying in your bed at night. Have your music ready and turn it on when you feel anxious.

I chill with my iPod

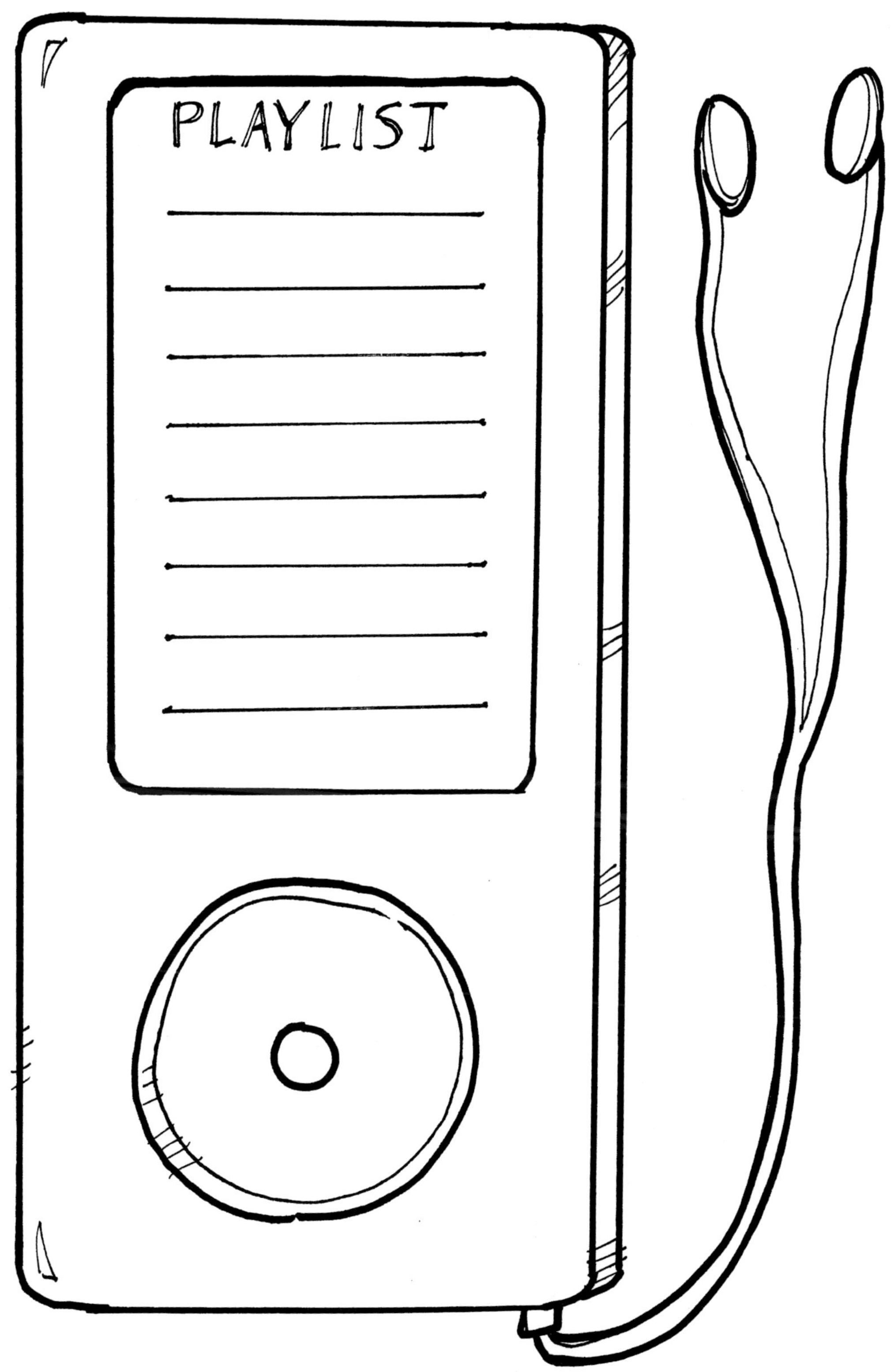

What are Your Worried Thoughts?

All the stories at the front of this book have one thing in common. They all have an enemy that speaks worried thoughts to them. These enemies represent the worried talk that we say to ourselves...it's just easier–and more fun–to fight them if we give them a face and a name. Daniel has a dragon that gets bigger and bigger the more he listens to it, Polly has Princess Perfect and Oscar has a clinging octopus.

The first step in fighting our worried thoughts is to know what they are. The next several pages give you lots of ways to get these worried thoughts down on paper. First, there's a worried brain. Some kids like to use this to write down their worried thoughts. If you like the story of Daniel, you can record your worried thoughts on the dragon flames. If Princess Perfect seems more like your kind of enemy, you can record your worried thoughts on her wand. Oscar the Octopus even has his worried thoughts started with "What if..." If none of these are quite right for you, you can create your own worry creature and write down what it tells you.

The Worried Brain

Fill in each section of the brain with one of your worried thoughts.

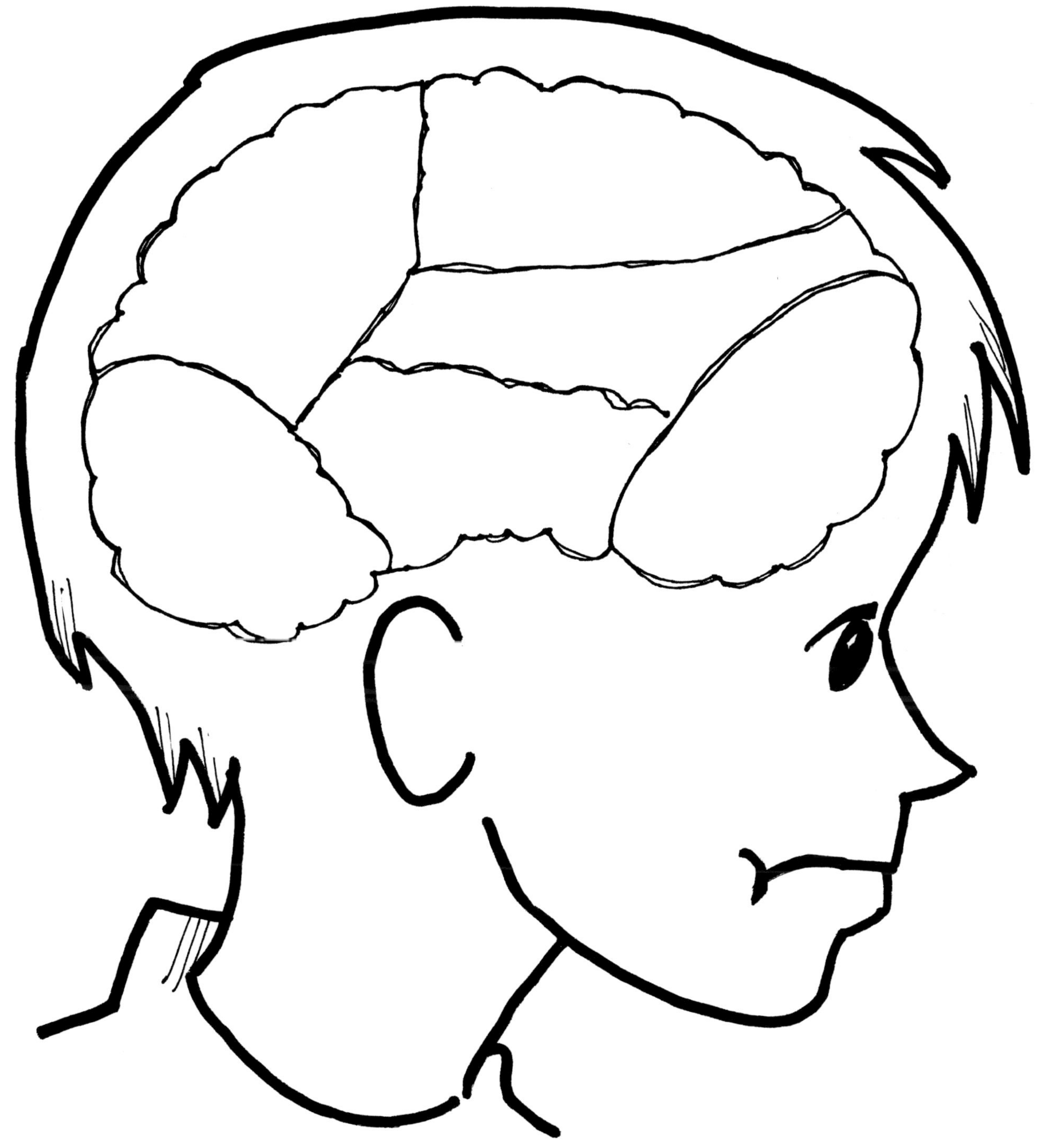

Draw your own dragon

The Dragon's Flames

Daniel's dragon attacked him with fiery worried talk. Use these flames to write down the worried talk that your dragon tells you.

Draw your own princess

The Princess Wand

Princess Perfect used her wand to make Polly feel bad. Write the things your princess says to you on the wand below.

Draw your own clinging creature

Thought Stopping

Thought Stopping

Once you have written down the worried talk you can practice silencing it. At first it may be hard to stop the worried talk from repeating, but as you practice, it will become easier.

Cut out and color the traffic hand to remind you to stop the worried talk when it starts.

Getting *Stronger*

Have your helpful adult say the worried talk outloud. Each time you hold up the traffic hand, the grown up has to stop speaking immediately. It's even more fun to blow a whistle as you hold up the stop sign. The sharp whistle blast stops the worried talk right away.

Thought Stopping

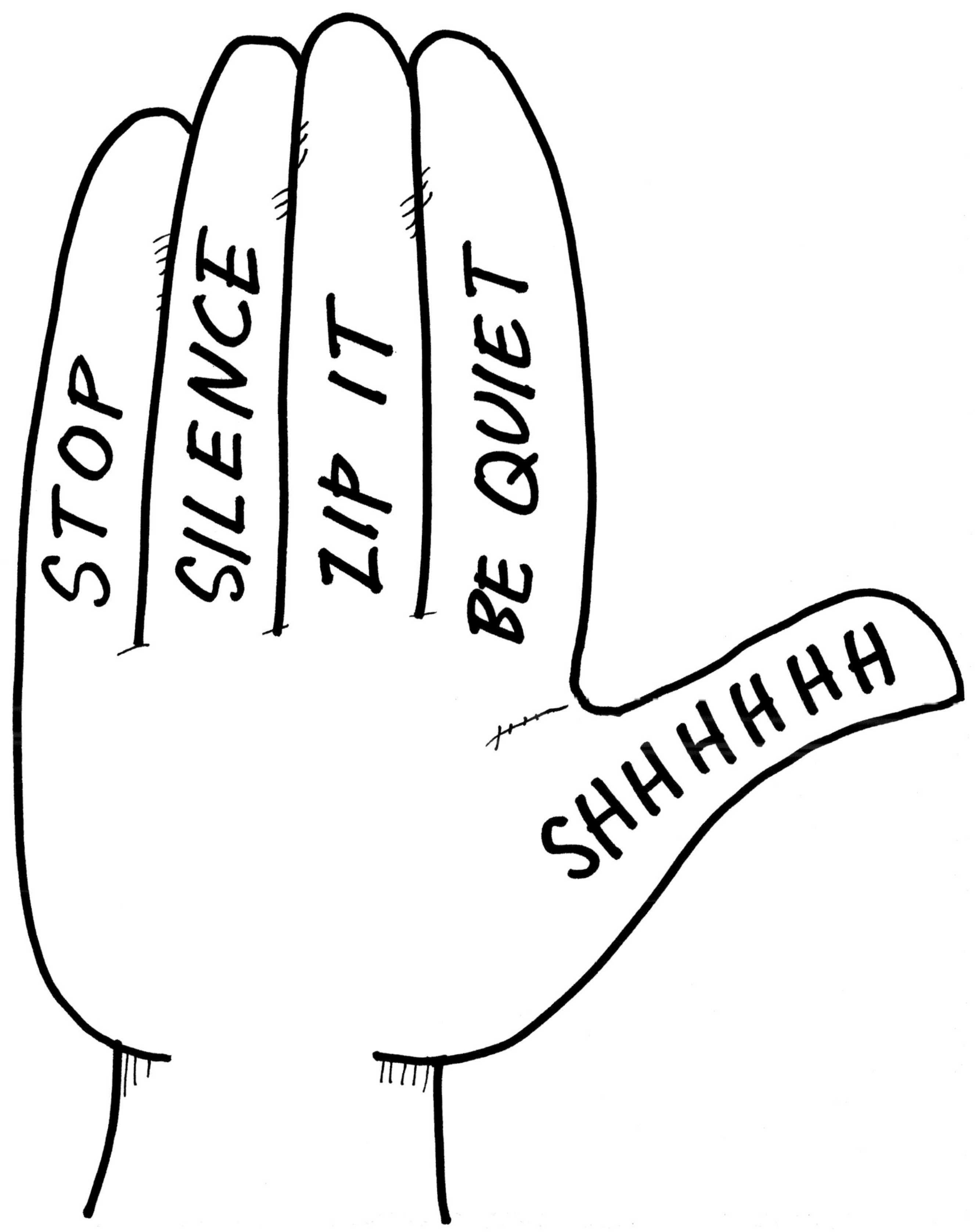

Bossing Back the Worried Talk

So far, your worry creature has you believing that it's the boss. You've got to show it who's really the boss. Using the boss back words that you will make up on the following pages can help.

Some kids like to argue with their worry creature. Others like to ignore it. Still others like to persuade or teach the creature that it doesn't have to worry so much.

How you fight back is up to you, *but you must fight back.*

Getting *Stronger*

Once you have written down your boss back talk on the following pages, it can be fun to practice saying them with toy weapons. Have your helpful adult repeat the creature's worried talk while throwing balls at you. You will have a sword and a shield and must practice your boss back words while protecting yourself from the flying balls!

The Boss Back Brain

Fill in each section of the brain with one thing you can say to boss back the worried talk.

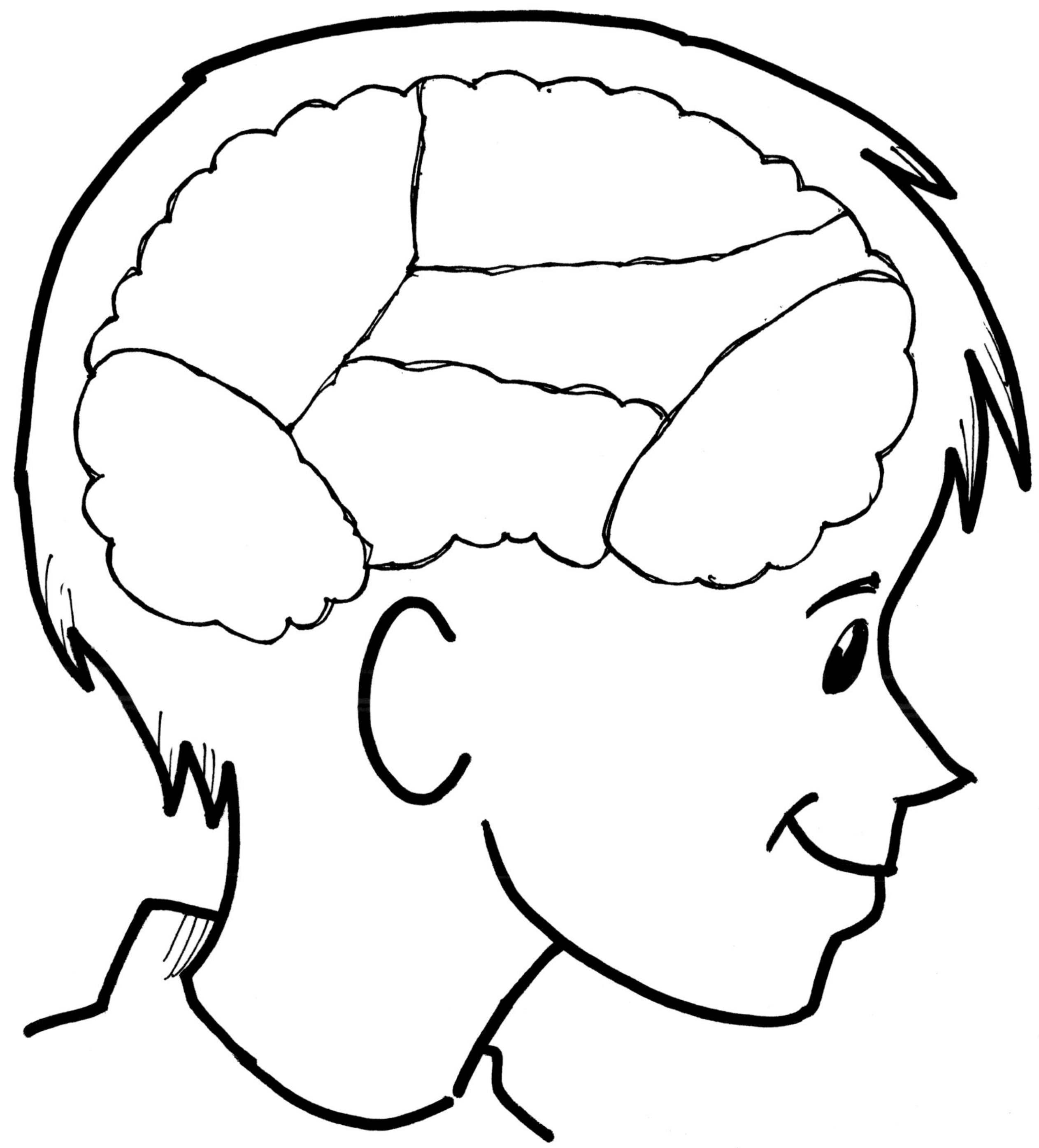

The Sword

Come up with some things you can say to talk back to your worry creature. Write each one on a part of the sword, cut it out and keep it nearby as a reminder of the power you have to fight back.

Getting *Stronger*

The Sword

The Shield

Shields offer protection during an attack. They can also deflect the worried talk that your creature says to you.

In each of the four sections of this shield, write one thing you can say to talk back to your worry creature.

Getting *Stronger*

The shield can also be a reminder of how your family helps you fight the worry wars. Family unity is a powerful weapon. You and your family can come up with one or more symbols that show how you are a unified front and draw them in the shield of your choosing.

The Shield

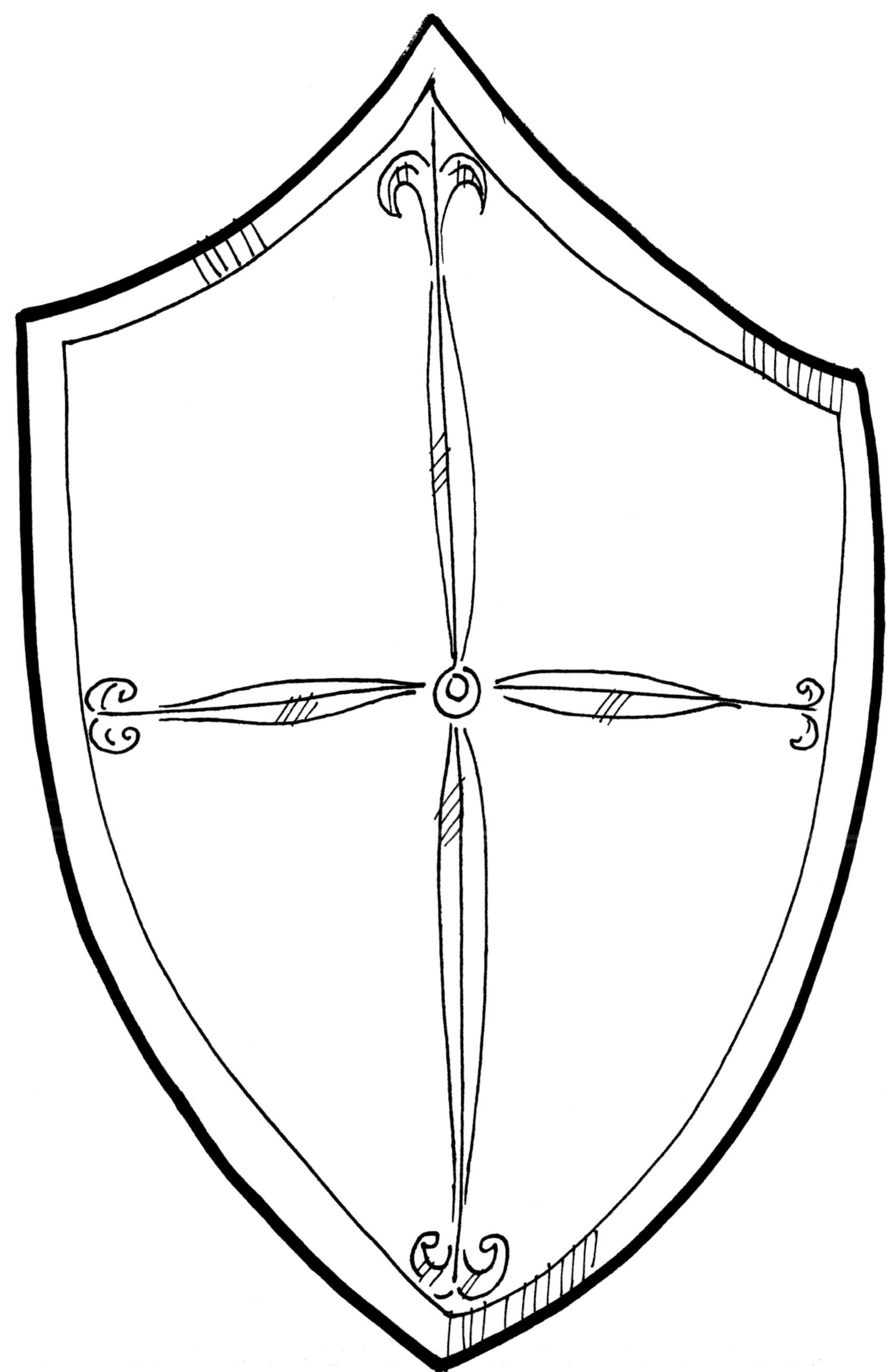

The Shield

Use these shields to draw symbols of things you can do when the worried talk starts, or write things you can say to boss back the worry creature.

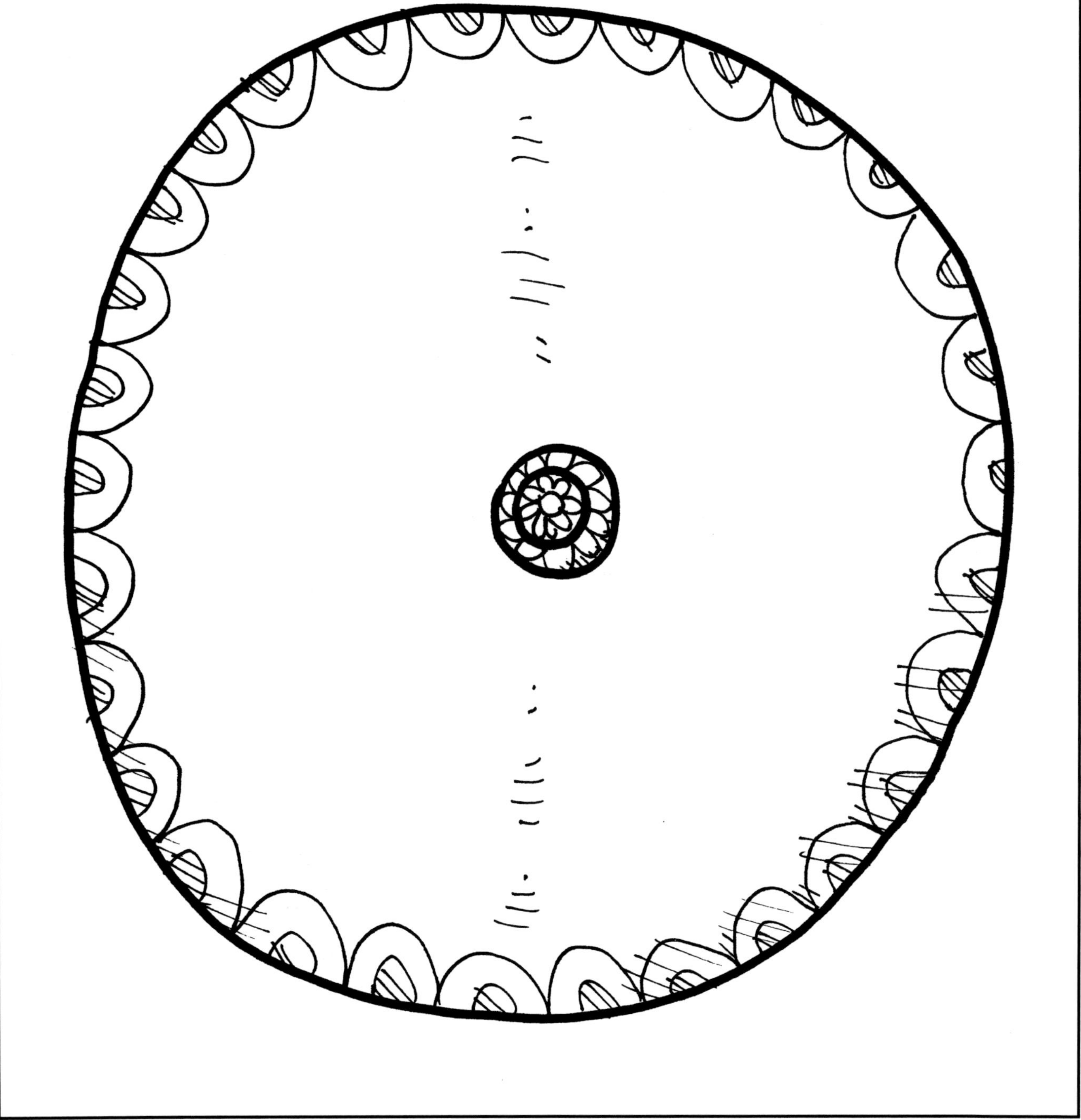

The Shield

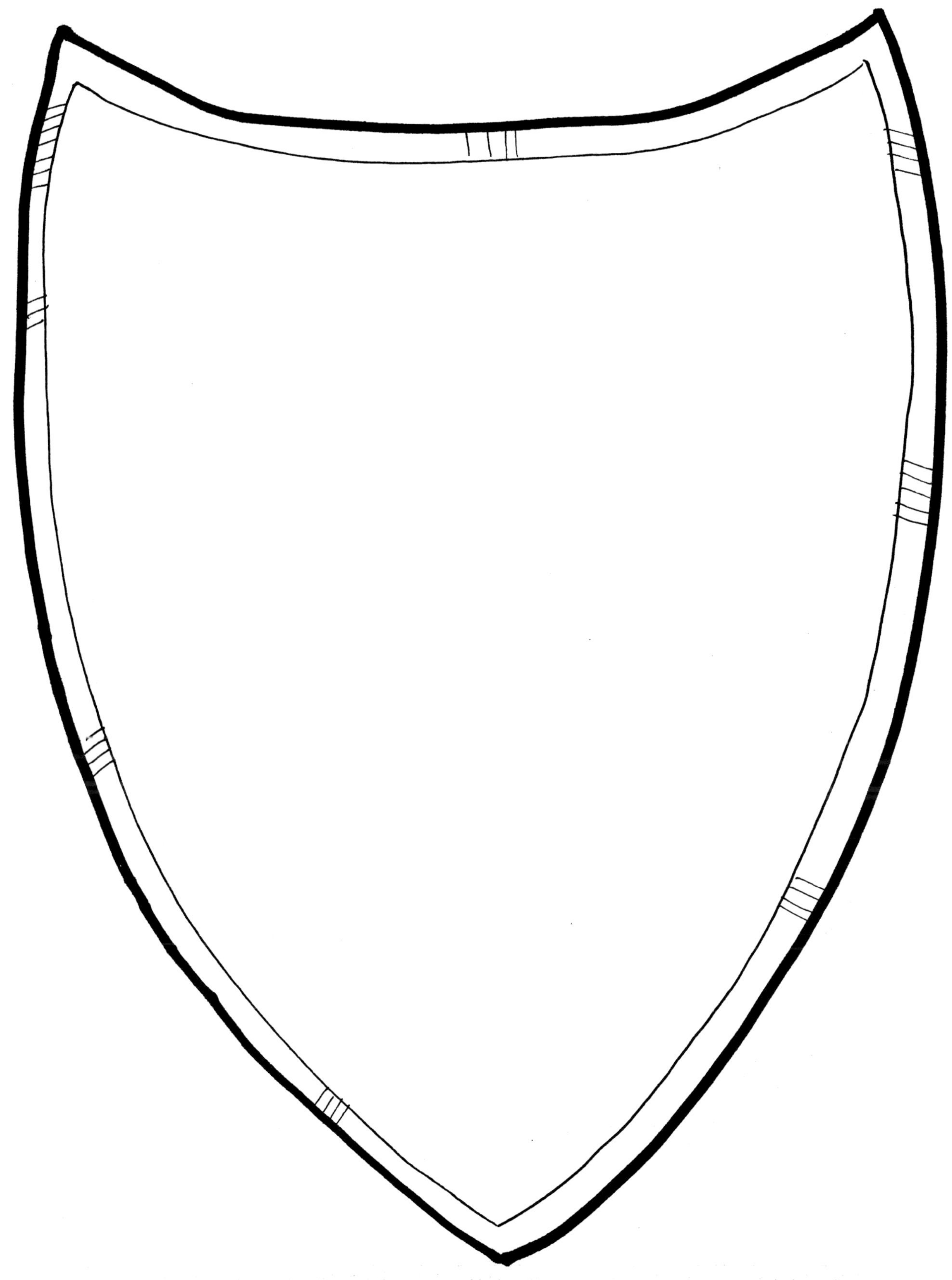

Extinguish the Flames

In "Daniel the Dragon Slayer," Daniel finally extinguishes the dragon's fiery breath by using a fire extinguisher. Here's your very own fire extinguisher.

On the canister of the fire extinguisher, write in big words your best argument against the dragon's worried talk. Cut it out and keep it nearby to remember your boss back words.

Getting *Stronger*

Draw a picture of your worry creature on a dry erase board. Then use a play fire extinquisher or a spray bottle of water and spray the board as you practice your boss back talk. One swipe of a paper towel and your worry creature is gone! You an also use a piece of regular paper. The worry creature will get soaked and be easy to rip up!

Extinguish the Flames

The Megaphone

Polly finally gets rid of Princess Perfect by using her sister's megaphone. She talks back to the Princess and the megaphone gives her words such force that she blows Princess Perfect right out the window.

Use the megaphone on the opposite page to write down things you would like to say to Princess Perfect. Cut it out, decorate it and keep it close to remind you of your boss back talk.

Getting *Stronger*

Make a real megaphone out of large construction paper. Have your helpful adult be the voice of the Princess (or other worry creature) and practice using your boss back talk through the megaphone!

The Megaphone

The Winning Wand

In the story, Polly waited until Princess Perfect was asleep and took away her Worry Wand. Here you can make your own wand, filling it with positive statements about yourself or phrases like "I'm good enough." You can even tell the Princess to leave you alone.

There aren't many times when it's appropriate to call someone a liar, but if you called Princess Perfect a liar, you would simply be telling the truth.

Getting *Stronger*

Make edible magic wands as a fun snack with your helpful adult. First make peanut butter and jelly sandwiches and use a heart shaped cookie cutter to cut them into star shapes. Then insert a long pretzel rod into the middle. Voila! Practice bossing back Princess Perfect while you share this snack together.

The Winning Wand

THE BATTLES

The Battlefield

Yeah you! Give yourself a pat on the back for the hard work that you've already done to get ready for the battle. You learned what worry is and how it gets bigger when you feed it. You've learned how worry tries to take over your body, and you've developed strategies for taking control of your body back. You've learned how worried thoughts try to take over your mind and you've developed strategies to recapture your thoughts. You've gathered a team of support people and learned ways to cope and stay strong as you fight your fears.

Now you're ready for the next step.

The Strategy of the Enemy

When you're trying to win a war, it helps to understand the strategy of your enemy. When you feel worried, your body gets upset and your worry creature tells you to avoid (or get away from) the situation that is making you feel worried. As soon as you get away from the thing that worries you, you feel better. Your body calms down, and the worried talk get softer ... for a minute.

Here comes the tricky part. You'll feel better briefly when you avoid the things that you're worried about, but pretty soon the worried talk comes back stronger, louder, bigger than before! Avoiding the thing that makes you worried feeds the worry!

The Solution

It's really too bad, but the only way to gain control over your worry is to do the thing that makes you worried *anyway*.

Your worry creature will always tell you to avoid the thing that makes you anxious. The lie that your worry creature tells you is that when your worry alarm starts to go off, you should move away from the thing that makes you worried. The lie is a pretty good one because *you do feel better for a minute* ... but here's the tricky part ... and once you know this, you know the key to beating your worry creature ... *you only feel better for a minute*. Then the next time the worried talk comes, you have to work harder and run faster to get away from your worry. Eventually, you end up a slave to your worries.

One Battle at a Time

So, where do you start? Where do you draw the battle line?

When fighting your fears, it's wise to start small. If your worry is centered around "one big thing" like going to school, don't try to do that one big thing on the first day of the war. Instead, plan out some things you can do as baby steps in the right direction.

For example, your first battle might be sitting next to mom and imagining yourself walking into school and waving goodbye. Your second battle might be driving to school and sitting in the parking lot while imagining going in the building. Your third battle might be getting out of the car, walking inside the building for one minute and coming back out to the car to go home. Each time you are successful, your body and mind get stronger and your worry weakens.

The Pyramid

You want to start with something simple. Start with the easier trials and work up to things that are harder. For example, if you're afraid of being away from your parent, your first battle might be making yourself stay in a separate room for one or two minutes. Then work your way up to longer amounts of time.

Choose something that you know you can do and write it on the bottom of your pyramid. Having success in your first few battles will teach your body that you can do it!

The Pyramid

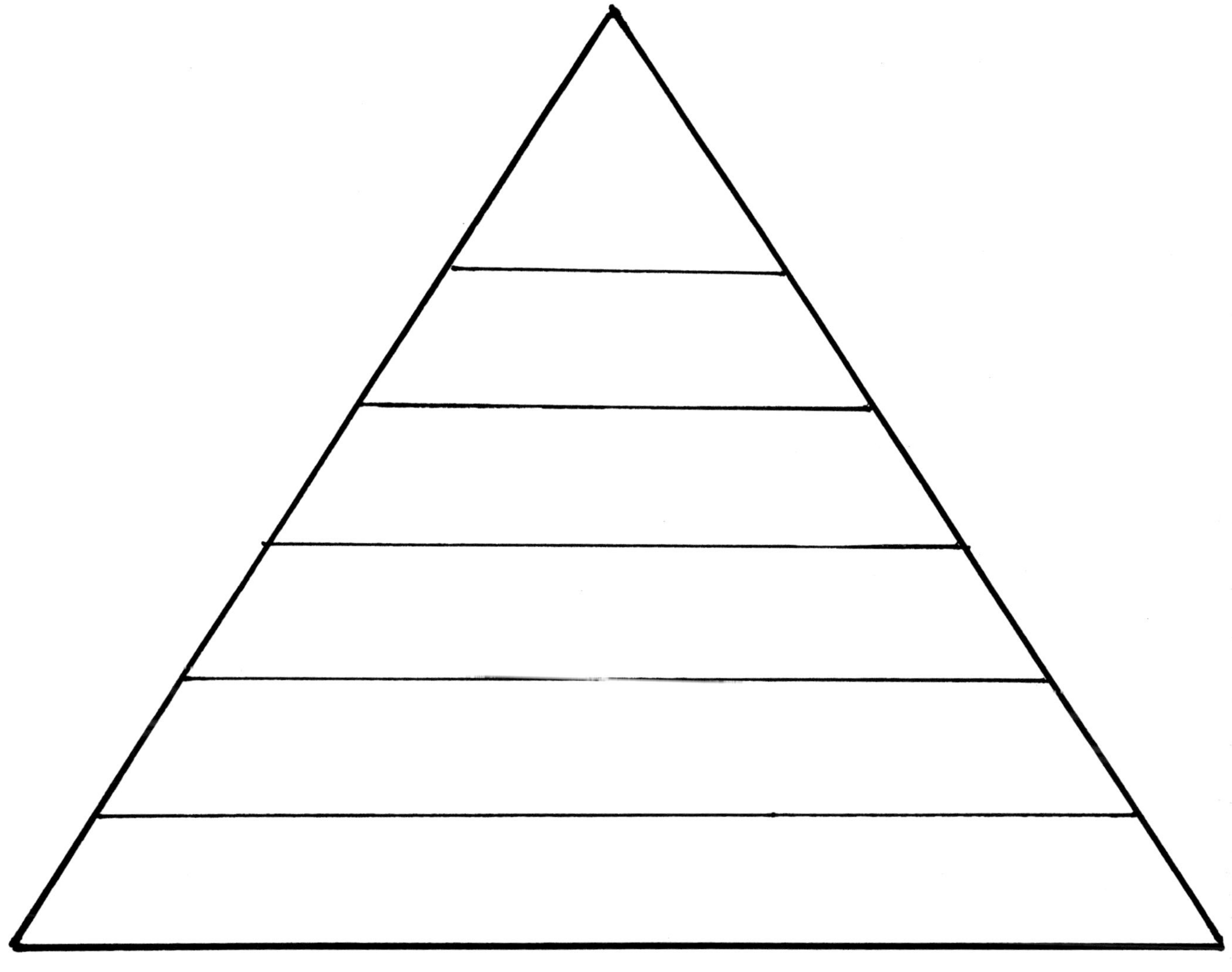

Paying Attention to How You Feel

The next few pages offer tools that help you track how bad you feel before you do something scary and how bad you feel soon after you've finished doing the scary thing.

The trickiest part of fighting your worried creature is pushing through the time when it gets loudest. You will often feel your very worst just before you do the thing that makes you anxious. The worry creature will lie to you and make you feel miserable, almost like you're going to die if you follow through. Strangely, a few minutes after you do the thing, you may feel almost normal again. Tracking how bad you feel before and after you've done the scary thing can help you see the lies of the enemy.

You're not going to die if you do the scary thing. In fact, soon after you do it, you may feel better than you've felt in a long time.

How bad does it feel?

On the next page you will see a set of feeling faces and a scale from 0 to 10. Each time you fight another battle, choose a number to express how bad you felt just *before* you did the scary thing and another that shows how bad you felt a couple of minutes *after* you did the scary thing. Write these numbers on whichever tracking tool you choose: the mountain, the ladder or the staircase.

The Feeling Faces Scale

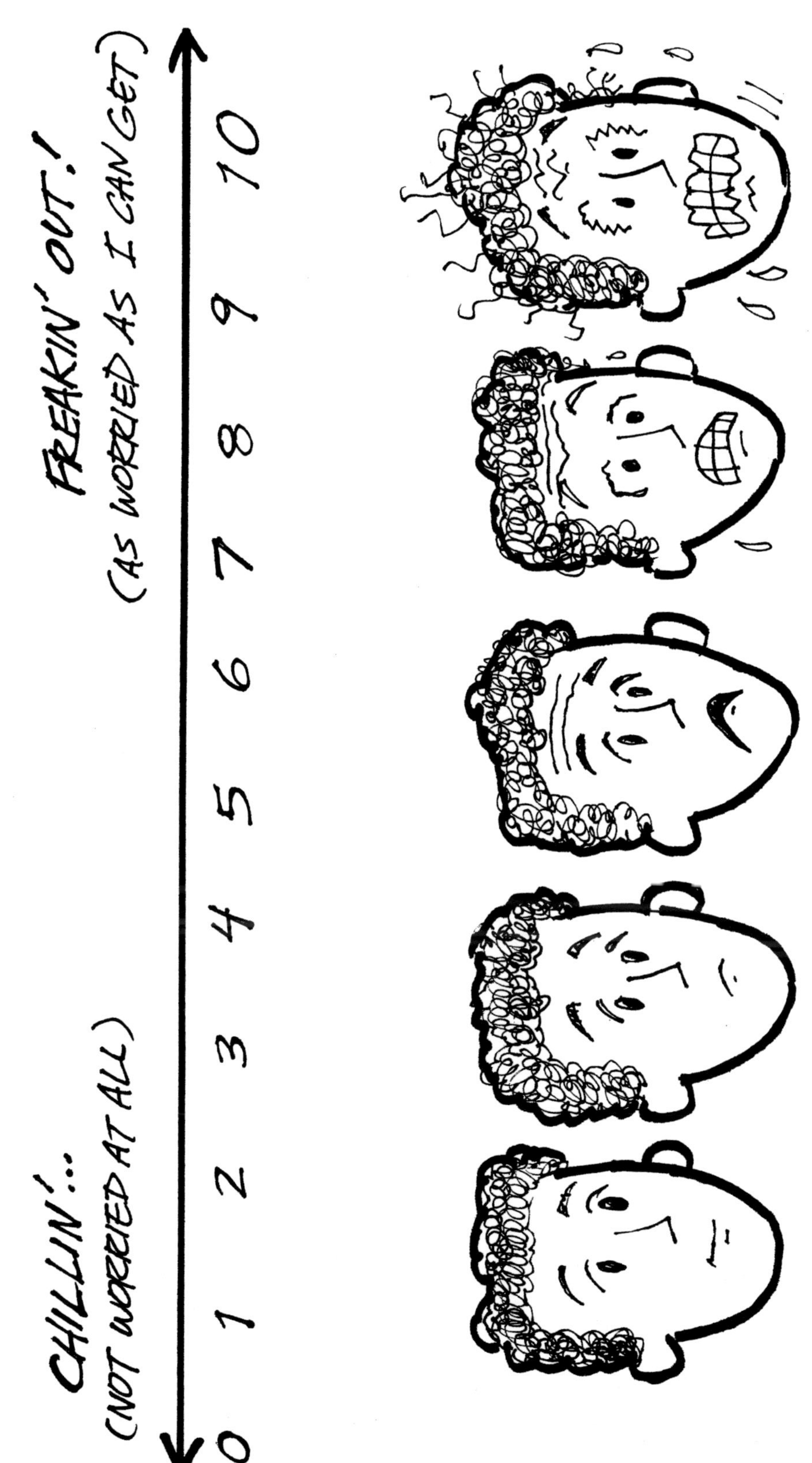

The Thermometer

Here's another way to track how bad you feel just before you do the scary thing and how you feel a few minutes after you've successfully done the scary thing. Just as the temperature on a thermometer rises as heat goes up, the numbers on this thermometer increase the more upset you feel.

The Thermometer

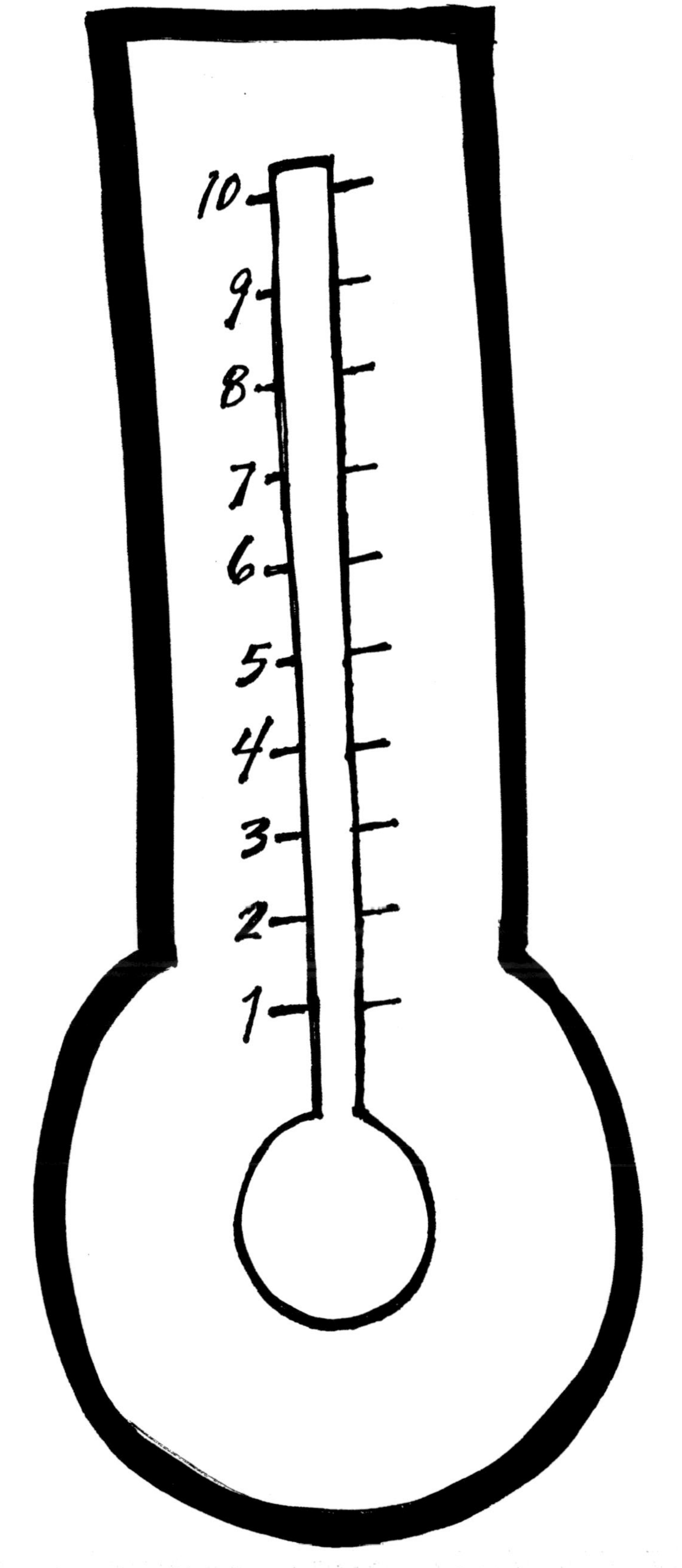

One-A-Day Thermometers

This is a whole week's worth of thermometers to help you track how bad you feel before and after your battles. Draw an "B" on the thermometer to show how bad you felt before doing the scary thing. Draw an "A" on the same thermometer to show how bad you felt two to three minutes after doing the scary thing.

Try to do one scary thing each day. For each thermometer that you mark, you will get a reward from your helpful adult.

One-A-Day Thermometers

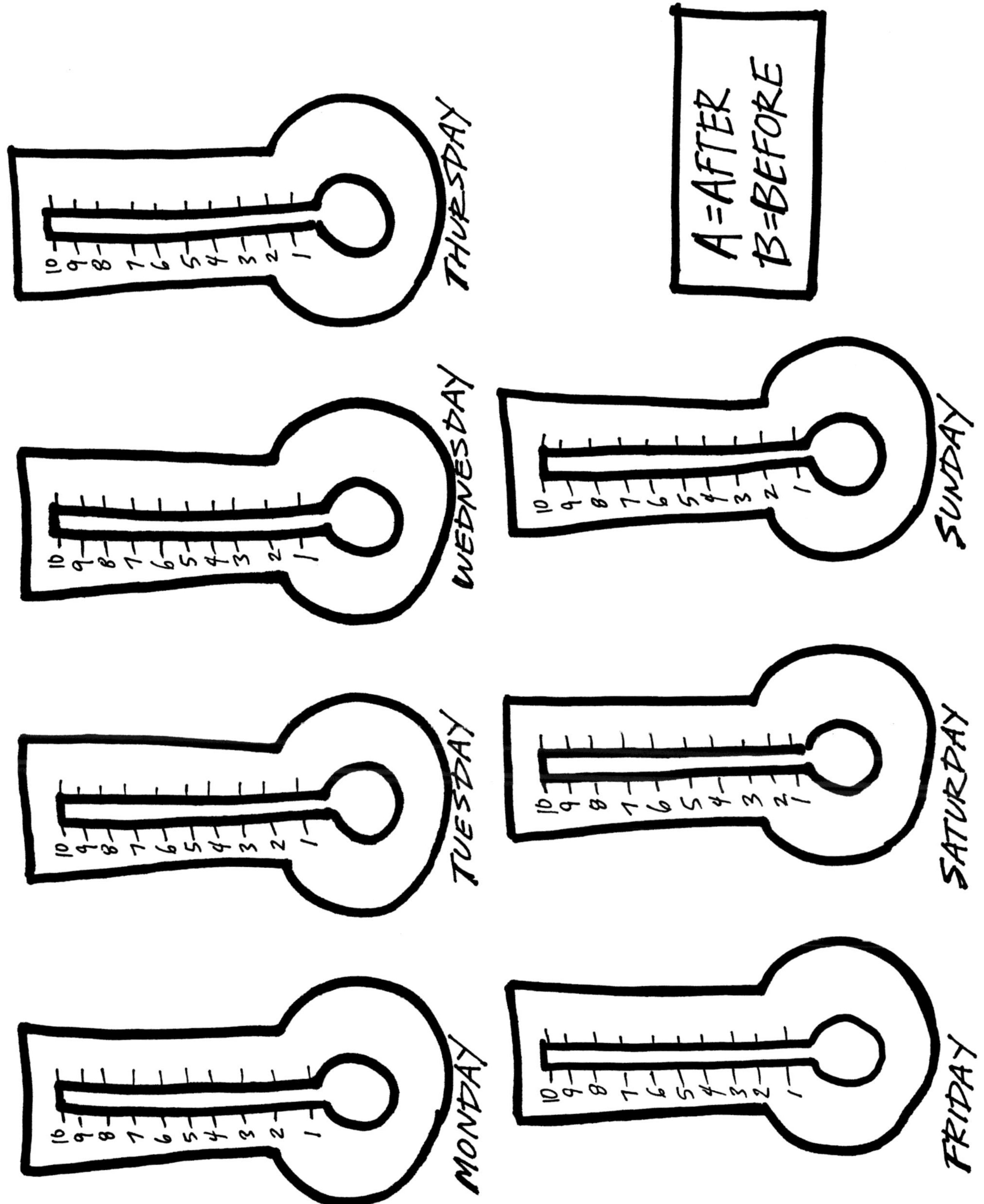

Storing Up Treasure

Fighting your battles can be hard work. It's nice to be rewarded for hard work. Ask your helpful adult to join you in coming up with some small rewards that you can receive each time you fight one of your battles. A small reward would be a piece of candy, a plastic ring, a cool eraser or other small treasure box item. Small daily rewards can also include special activities like getting to stay up ten minutes past your normal bedtime, getting fifteen minutes of extra computer time, or reading an extra book before bed. On each of the four coins pictured in front of the treasure chest on the next page write down one of the small rewards that you and your helpful adult have agreed upon.

After you've recorded a whole page of successful battles, you can choose a bigger reward. Bigger rewards might include a trip to the ice cream store or the movie theater,or the purchase of a special toy you've been hoping to have. Agree together with your helpful adult on the rewards you can earn and write them in the two diamond shaped treasures on the next page.

Storing Up Treasure

Step-By-Step

The staircase on the next page is one way to track your successes. Each time that you do the thing that makes you anxious anyway, you can record it on a step in the staircase. You can also put a sticker on that stair to show that you're making progress. Each time you fill in a step you get another small reward and you get closer to winning the war.

When you have filled in all ten steps, you can draw a picture of yourself smiling at the top! Filling in all the steps earns you the bigger reward that you and your helpful adult agreed to.

Getting *Stronger*

You can also make a staircase out of clay and track your successes that way. Toothpicks with flags can be inserted into each step as you fight another battle.

When you get to the top, celebrate!

The Staircase

The Mountain

Each time that you are afraid to do something and you do it anyway, write your success on each step up the mountain. You get a small reward for each of your successes. Decide on a bigger reward that you can enjoy when you have gotten all the way to the top of the mountain.

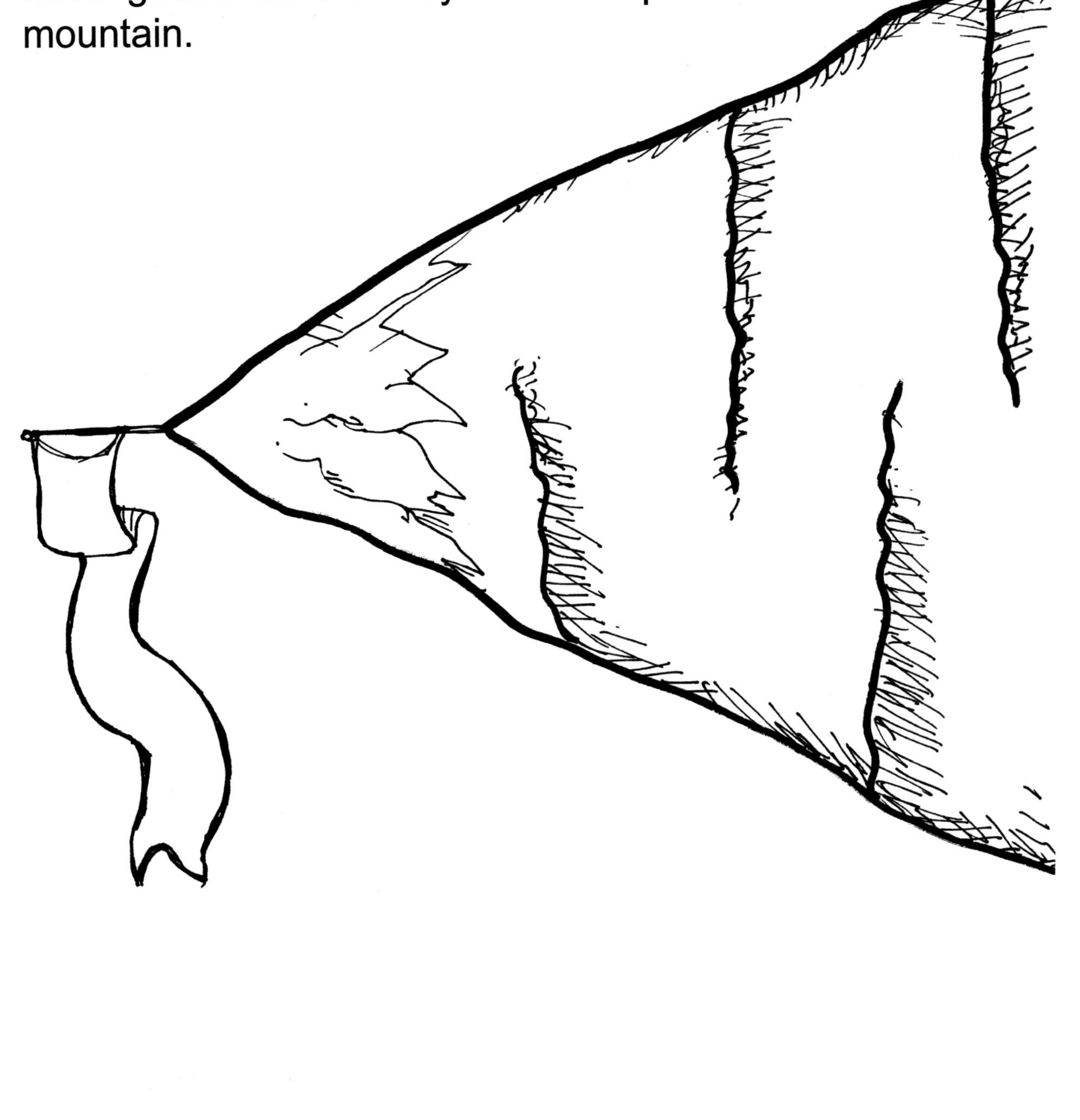

The Mountain

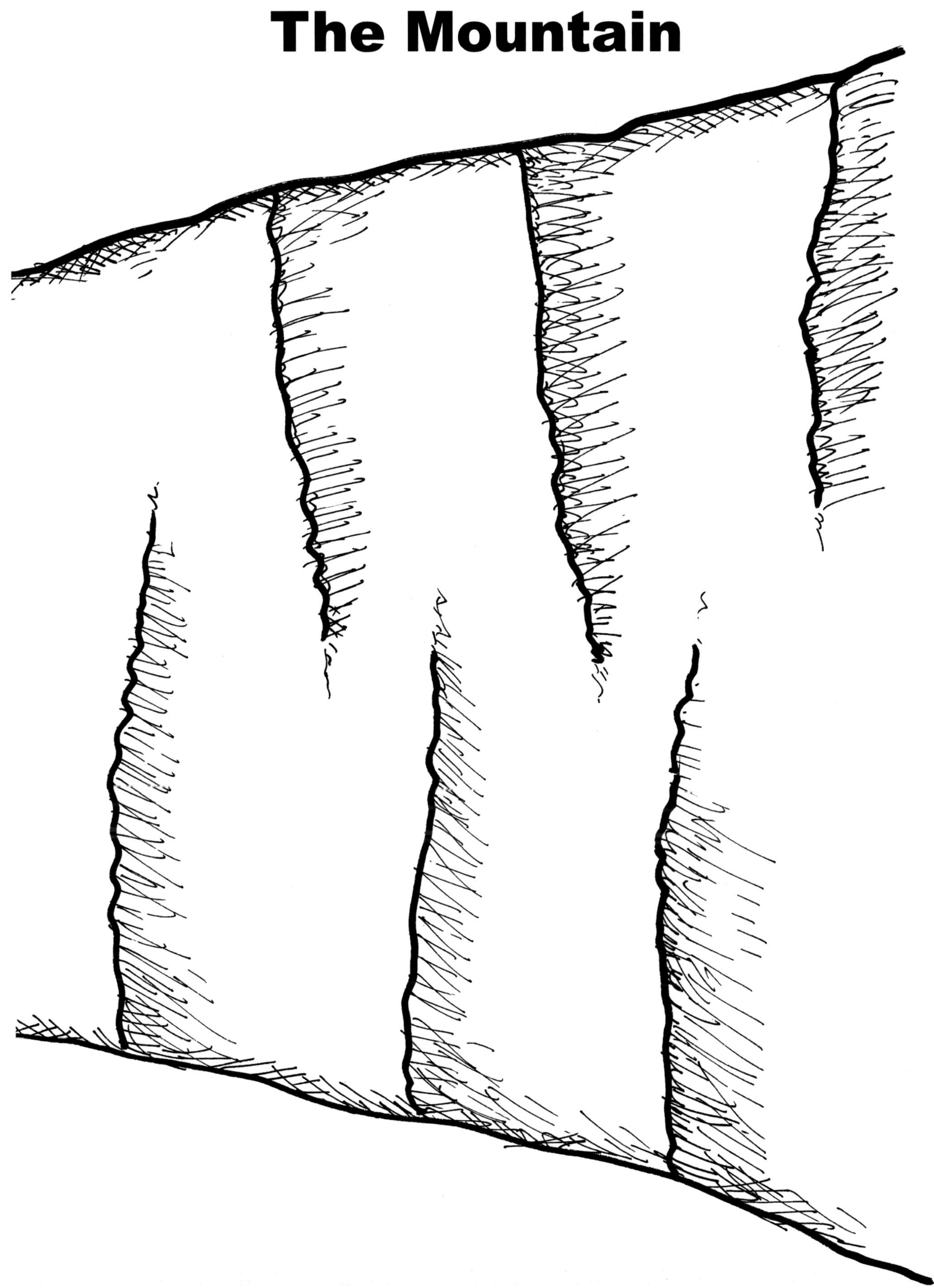

The Ladder

Each time that you are afraid to do something and you do it anyway, write your success inside one of the rungs of the ladder. You get a small reward for each of your successes. Decide on a bigger reward that you can enjoy when you have filled in every rung on the ladder.

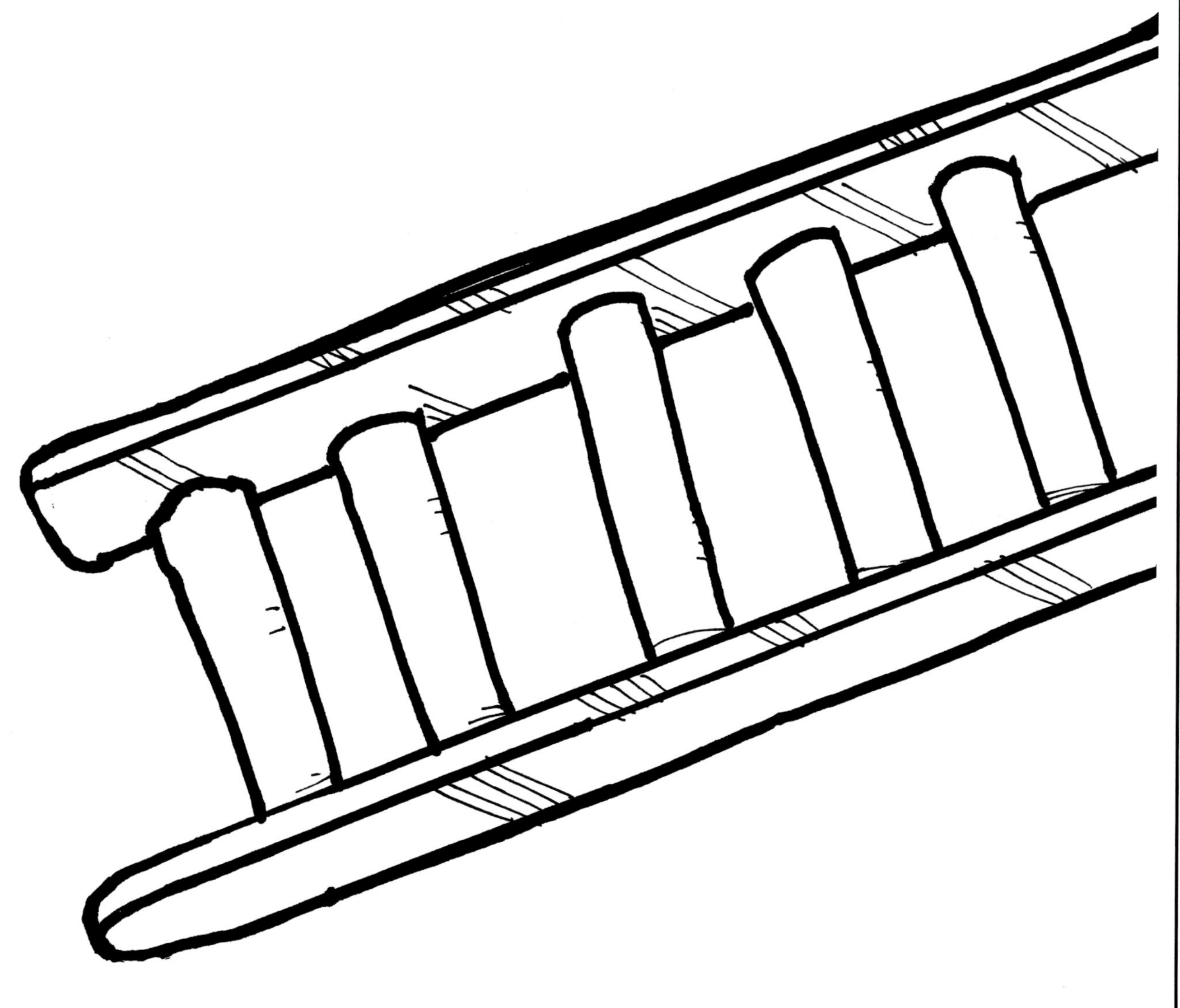

The Ladder

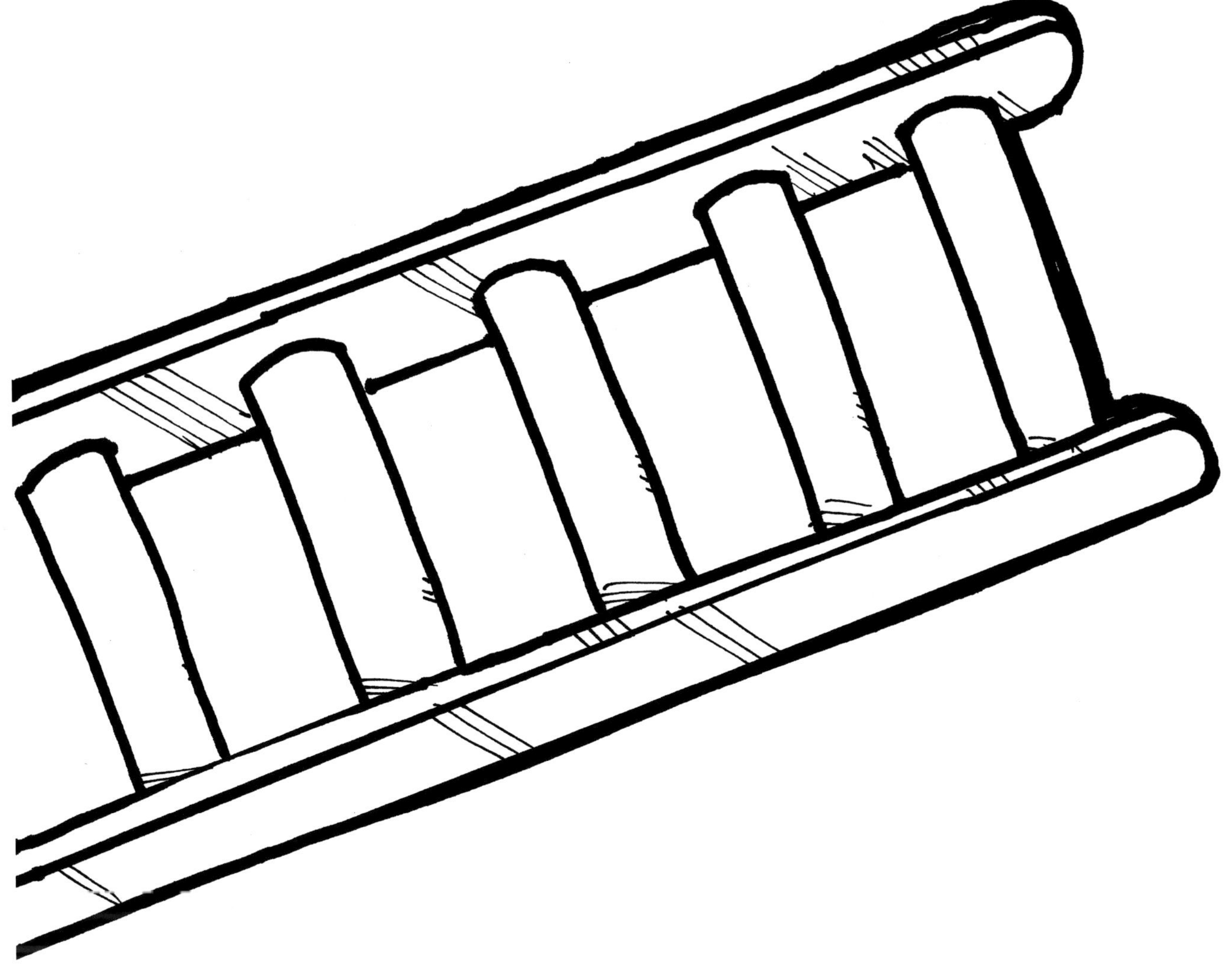

The Creature Cover-Up

Use the bricks on the next page to cover up your worry creature. Copy the bricks onto red construction paper and cut them out. Choose one of the creatures from the stories or create your own creature. Each time you fight a worry battle, choose a brick and glue it over a part of your worry creature. Each brick earns you a small reward.

You can write a variety of boss back statements on the bricks, or write down what you did to win each battle. Pretty soon the creature will be completely covered up and you can celebrate with your helpful adult.

The Bricks

Make Them Disappear!

On each of these next three pages are full size drawings of the dragon, Princess Perfect, and Clyde the Clinging Octopus. You can cut these out and cover them with bricks, or each time you beat back your worry, you can rip a piece off of the creature you choose and trade it in for a reward. In this way, you can watch your worry creature literally disappear!

The Dragon

I am yours to do with what you will. You can cover me up with bricks or you can cut me out and rip pieces off of me each time you win a battle. You can also make a puppet out of me and have live rehearsals for the battles or live reenactments after each time you've beaten me!

Princess Perfect

I am yours to do with what you will. You can cover me up with bricks or you can cut me out and rip pieces off of me each time you win a battle. You can also make a puppet out of me and have live rehearsals for the battles or live reenactments after each time you've beaten me!

Clyde, the Clinging Octopus

I am yours to do with what you will. You can cover me up with bricks or you can cut me out and rip pieces off of me each time you win a battle. You can also make a puppet out of me and have live rehearsals for the battles or live reenactments after each time you've beaten me!

Draw Your Worry Creature

Daniel

This full size version of Daniel can be used to create a puppet. Simply cut him out and paste him on a paper bag or glue him to a popsicle stick. He can be used in role plays to fight the dragon. He can practice relaxation, rehearse his boss back talk, or celebrate victories.

Polly

This full size version of Polly can be used to create a puppet. Simply cut her out and paste her on a paper bag or glue her to a popsicle stick. She can be used in role plays to fight Princess Perfect. She can practice relaxation, rehearse her boss back talk, or celebrate victories.

Oscar

This full size version of Oscar can be used to create a puppet. Simply cut him out and paste him on a paper bag or glue him to a popsicle stick. He can be used in role plays to fight Clyde, the Clinging Octopus. He can practice relaxation, rehearse his boss back talk, or celebrate victories.

THE VICTORY

Guard Against New Worries

You have bossed back your worried talk. Now you are in control of your worries instead of them being in control of you! However, new worries will always try to sneak in when you are least expecting them. It's the nature of worry.

A smart warrior will always be ready when new worries come. On the opposite page are some of the ways that new worries start. Circle the ways you are most likely to encounter new worries. You and your helpful adult can discuss strategies to use when new worries try to take hold.

Guard Against New Worries

You see something worrisome on the TV or on the computer.

You overhear some grown-ups talking about something scary.

You read something upsetting in a newspaper, book or magazine.

What will you do when you are presented with something new that you could worry about?

Freed Up Time

Now that you have bossed back your worries, your brain has more space for reading books, solving puzzles and other kinds of learning. Draw a picture of something fun you want to learn more about.

Freed Up Time

Now that you have bossed back your worries, your body has more energy. Draw a picture of something fun you can do with your body.

Graduation

You've made it! You've won the worry wars and now it's time to celebrate! You can plan a graduation ceremony to mark the occasion. On the next page is a graduation invitation.

You and your helpful adult can make a list of important people to invite. On the next page is an invitation that you can copy and hand out to guests.

Getting *Stronger*

Ask the adults who helped you fight the worry wars to write letters about the progress they've seen you make. These letters can be brought to the celebration and read out loud. You can keep these letters and bring them out to read whenever you need a little encouragement. Also,plan special food and decorations for your graduation celebration.

Graduation Invitation

Thanking Your Helpful Adults

Decide which you like better, the trophy or the ribbon, for each helpful adult on your team. Make as many copies of each as you need. On each award, write the name of your team member and one way that person helped you to conquer your worries. Decorate these awards and give them out at your party!

Thanking Your Helpful Adults

Graduation Hat

You have learned a whole lot about how worry works and the best ways to fight it. Using the graduation hat on the next page, write in two of the most important things you learned about how to fight your worries.

Getting *Stronger*

You and your helpful adult can make a graduation hat out of cardboard or construction paper. Use the top of the hat to record lessons you learned about fighting your worries. On the band that sits on your head, write something about how strong you've gotten. You can make the tassle out of several pieces of yarn tied together. For each piece of yarn in your tassle, say something nice about yourself.

Graduation Hat

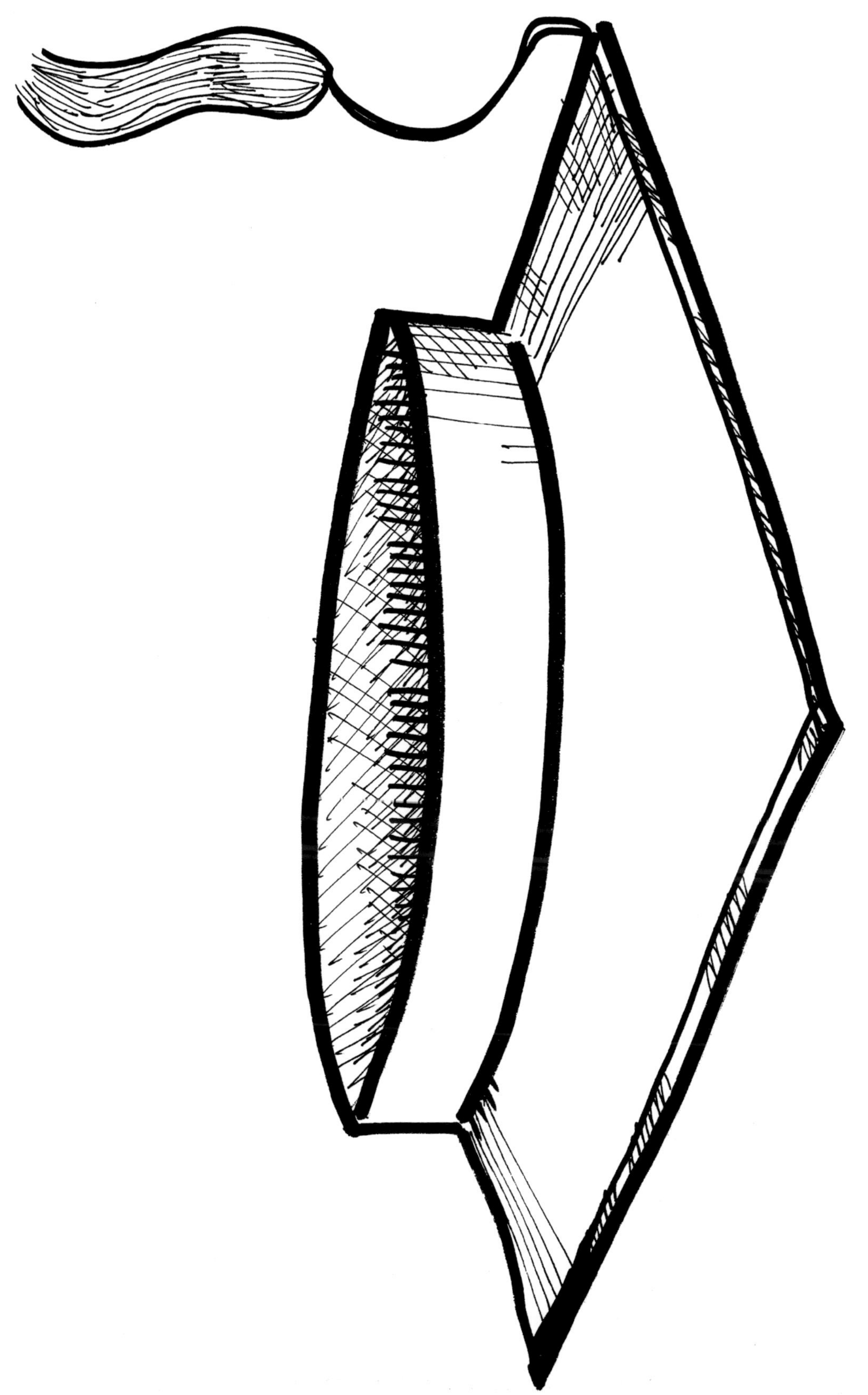

Graduation Diploma

The graduation diploma on the next page can be copied off and filled in during your graduation ceremony. Hang it on your wall and when new worries come your way, it will serve as a great reminder that you have everything you need to beat them back again!

You and your helpful adult can fill in your name, the date, and then each of you can sign at the bottom, just like you would on any official document!

Getting *Stronger*

You and your helpful adult can spend time making a frame for your diploma. Decorate it any way you want, but leave room around the edges for team members to write nice things about you!

Graduation Diploma